HEALING MANTRAS

VERDA HARPER

CONTENTS

PART II

This checklist includes:

- 10 ways to prepare for the successful use of healing with Mantras and Chakras.
- The highest quality items.
- Where you can buy these items for the lowest price.

The last thing we want is for your healing start to be delayed because you weren't as prepared as you could be.

To receive your checklist, visit the link:

INTRODUCTION

It was over five years ago when a somewhat eccentric friend of mine started raving about a spiritualist she had visited. After two sessions, my friend had become an expert on mantras and was determined to use spiritual healing to transform her life.

As with anyone who takes up a new interest, she went on about how I need to do this and that. She could see the darkness of my aura and warned me that I needed to do something about it. I giggled a little and assumed it would be another passing phase she was going through.

At first, I admit I wasn't too keen to delve into the depths of the subject, probably because of the way my friend was portraying her new passion. We would be out for coffee and she would lay her healing crystals out and start chanting things that only she could understand. Along with a few "Oms" and "Shanti" (which I later learnt means peace in Pali, an Indian language), the only thing she seemed to achieve was some strange stares from the adjacent tables.

So, as I was trying to convince my friend that mantras were not going to transform her life, I found that they would transform mine. I read one quote that hit me with such an impact.

"The quieter the mind, the more you can hear"

— ANONYMOUS

There was nothing complex about the theory, but when I tried to put it into practice, I simply couldn't. My mind was racing with things I had to do, worries, and problems. It was impossible to break from the hectic world. But I loved the idea so much, I had to learn how to do it.

Needless to say, my friend's interest soon faded as she moved on to tarot cards, a whole other experience which I have also dedicated a book to. But I must thank her because it was her experience that led me to begin my spiritual journey. Like many, I thought that the concept of spirituality was a bit of a con and looking back this is probably because of how it has been commercialized. Every time I made the awful journey into the hectic city, I would pass a holistic shop with dream catchers covering the windows. Aside from never having the time, there was something that was putting me off going in. Long-haired mysterious women with healing powers have appeared in numerous films and have become a stereotype far from reality. My interest began by trying to poke holes in the concept. The complete opposite happened as I started to see the great sense in the original teachings, the parts that we rarely see on films and TV.

It wasn't that I was unhappy with my life. I was blessed with two amazing children and a husband who worked hard so that I could stay at home to be with the kids. However, there was something off, something missing. I was stuck in a rut, mentally and physically. Being a mum is the best job in the world but there comes a point when you lose your sense of being and struggle to find purpose in your life.

This is the point that I had reached. Every mother will be able to relate to this at some point, but it felt like my destiny featured a hoover and several loads of washing. I fell into depression, unhealthy habits and a lack of interest in the world. I knew something had to be done and I wanted to better my life. But I wasn't sure that Western traditions were the right solution for me.

I realized that in order for me to change my life, I didn't need gimmicks or tricks, I needed guidance. I needed to find peace.

From this first quote, I saw that I would have to empty my mind of trivial things like household budgets and meal planning. This would allow me to truly hear what my mind and body required.

This quote started my thirst for learning. I became a student again, with a fresh notebook and a Google history filled with searches on Eastern philosophies. I was bursting with energy when I signed up for my first online course in Buddhism. In just a few short months, I felt like a different person and I had only scratched the surface.

I took up yoga and meditation. Neither of which was as easy as I had thought. I had become physically out of shape in my state of depression and after learning that yoga was far more than just a bit of stretching. The back ache that had prevented me from other exercise gradually eased as I found myself becoming physically fitter. I knew I was getting a better night's sleep because I wasn't waking up tired. I had more energy and with a little weight loss, I felt far more confident.

Meditation took time and effort to master, something that I will share with you throughout this book. Cleansing the mind brought about a new way of thinking for me and a higher level of clarity, but for someone whose brain is constantly interrupted, I had put in the effort to see the results.

These two practices are just a small part of my learning. I took to travelling so that I could gain first-hand insights from spiritual leaders and masters. I left no stone unturned. I read books and watched videos. I ignored what I felt to be too forced and followed gurus who didn't impose their teachings but instead, showed me the teachings so that I could draw my own conclusions.

While reading this book, I have 3 hopes. The first is that you are able to learn about mantras the same way I did and in no way pressurized. Second, I want you to gain understanding into the principles and philosophies going back to the earliest mantras in Vedic Sanskrit. My third hope is that together, we can work on removing negative thoughts in order for you to connect with your inner self and enhance the quality of your life.

Part of our educational path will be about how to create mantras that are meaningful to you as well as some of the most powerful mantras for various uses. We will discuss how to use mantras correctly so that you can refocus your mind, heal your body and realign your energies. I have chosen to include some recommendations for what not to do. As I have said, I don't want to impose my journey on you, but there are some lessons I wish I hadn't learnt over the years and I feel it's important to share them with you too.

If you have practised a little yoga or meditation and would like to take that to the next level, the information will allow you to build on you the knowledge you have. If you are feeling lost in life and have no experience in spiritualism, that is fine, there is no better place to start than here.

It is understandable if you are sceptical. You might be doubting just how far mantras can help you. Many have asked me "what if it does more harm than good?". Even more have felt that they aren't capable of healing, or they don't have time for spiritual practices. It's important that you realise that we can integrate mantras and healing into your daily life so that you can completely benefit from the positive changes that are about to occur. I too was full of self-doubt, but the philosophies have been practised for thousands of years for a good reason. You just need a pinch of faith.

Finally, I promise to make this an enjoyable experience for you. After all, introspection and self-realization can be an intense experience, so it's important for me to share my passion and learnings in a way that will put a smile on your face. I may even share the odd faux pas I have made along the way.

Nobody's life is the same. Some of us have high-demanding jobs, others are poor, some might be going through a divorce, mourning the loss of someone they loved, moving home, the list of our stresses and strains can go on. I am not here to compare my pains to yours or tell you that your problems can be fixed. One man's heaven is another man's hell and people view and handle problems differently. The one thing we have in common is that the problems you are suffering with are going to have a huge negative impact on your life, as did mine. What I aim to do is to guide you to a better life, the same way others have guided me. At the end of the day, we all need a little help sometimes, and this book is my help to you.

PART I

Not everyone will feel so eager to jump straight into the practice of mantras. Like many others, I needed time to explore the concepts and more than anything, I wanted to find out if there was any true of science behind the use of mantras for healing.

Your beliefs are reflected in your intentions, and your intentions are governed by your goals. On a larger scale, your goals are set depending on what you want from life. Every aspect of who you are will play a role in the mantras that you choose. At this point, and this is perfectly normal, you may have chosen this book without intentions or expectations, or you may have your heart set on changing something in your life that will then lead to even better things.

Because I was a sceptic at first, I wanted the focus of part 1 to be on the history of Hinduism and other Eastern philosophies. I want to share my passion for the Sanskrit language and why is it so important. I want to share my findings regarding the certain correlations between science and mantras. And we will begin to look and some mantras that can be used to prepare ourselves in order to get what we want from life.

Part 1 is like a history, science, and foreign language lesson from a teacher who never went to university but taught themselves through love of the subject and learning what works and what doesn't. The best thing is, although the lesson isn't compulsory, I am fairly sure you will get caught up in the fascinating complexities of healing mantras.

THE UNIVERSAL PRIMAL SOUNDS

I started my journey into mantras fairly early on into my spiritualism research. While I understood the theory behind them and even the science, it wasn't until I started practising yoga that I began to fully appreciate their meaning and power. The great thing is, you don't need to have any background in mantras to start benefiting from them. You don't need to be religious; you don't need to have a certain way of thinking. Mantras are used by students, businessmen, single mums, and everyone in between.

Hinduism and spiritual teachings are steeped in tradition and I feel that it is necessary to gain insight into the history of it to not only respect it but also to learn the intricate depths of the origins of mantras. For me, my experience was enhanced when I started to fit all of the puzzle pieces together. I realized how certain scriptures were used for different teaching methods, just like certain mantras were developed for certain purposes. I also grew to appreciate that it was how this knowledge was passed on throughout the centuries that impacts the effectiveness of the mantras and spiritual healing.

These are the areas we will focus on in this chapter. It's about learning the foundations in order to gain a higher sense of one's self. Equally important, is that while there is a religious side to Hinduism, there is also a side that doesn't call on the gods for enlightenment but requires a balance of the energies to lead you to the place you feel you want to need to be.

THE SOURCE OF HINDU KNOWLEDGE

To keep the ancient traditions alive, scriptures of Hindu texts were kept. Because the teachings are predominately oral, there is little information on the original author of the texts. They are considered to be a collaboration of teachings from both men and women and may have been added to with time.

These scriptures are either Shruti, to be heard, or Smriti, to be remembered. Vedas contain the most ancient of the Upanishads and are associated with meditation and spiritual knowledge and play a central role in Hinduism. The Vedas all fall under scriptures to be heard.

Upanishads- meaning by (upa) and ni-sad (sit down) or
Sitting down near"

There are 4 Vedas, all written in Vedic Sanskrit; Rigveda, Yajurveda, Samaveda, and Atharvaveda. Each contains a number of the 108 Upanishads.

Rigveda: This is a collection of 1,028 hymns and 10,600 verses that were composed between approximately 1500 and 1200 BCE. The teachings aim to answer questions regarding existence and are heavily based on universal vibrations.

Samaveda: The majority of the Samaveda was taken from Rigveda and then expanded with 75 mantras. Many of the scriptures were meant to be sung and were likely to have been danced to.

Yajurveda: The 1,875 verses are ritual offerings. There is a strong element of worship and religion in these teachings.

Atharvaveda: These scriptures also have elements of ritual offerings. There are around 760 hymns and 160 of those have similarities to teachings in Rigveda. It is composed of chants, hymns, and prayers that keep danger and evil at bay.

Each collection of Veda books contains four types of texts. They all have Aranyakas, texts of rituals and Brahmans, further interpretation of the rituals. Samhitas are the prayers and mantras within the Vedas. And that leads us back to the Upanishads, the philosophical works.

As you can see, Hinduism stands out from many religions because there is no one belief. There isn't one God that you must follow but instead, a collection of powerful rituals, chants and prayers. Some of the Hindu teachings are easier to master, others are complex and require time and practice. You will notice that not only are the scriptures and teachings different, but also the way in which knowledge is shared.

A STYLE OF LEARNING EMBEDDED IN TRADITION

There came a point when I had to move away from what I considered the best way to learn. As western tradition teaches us, we are accustomed to a student-teacher relationship where the teacher recites learned knowledge and the student takes down as many notes as possible to study later on.

I was basically the student and the teacher when it came to my research and I felt that I needed to write down mantras and learn them by heart. It was my first mistake, as I had pages of phrases with little pronunciation hints in the margin, but I didn't feel like anything was particularly sticking.

The student-teacher relationship in Hinduism is still an important one, but the dynamics are different. Mantras were handed down to students as say a grandmother would pass on her favourite recipe. She has practised her recipe over the years and doesn't need the ingredients to be written down. Her recipe is a part of her, like muscle memory.

Yogis have great wisdom which has come from the teachings they received and the experience that those teachings have given them. Knowledge is not forced on you but rather offered. As the student, you need to take the parts of the teachings that relate to you. And this is the same with mantras.

Across all of the Vedas, there are 20,379 mantras. Not everyone is going to be necessary for your healing. Some may be relevant for a part of your life while others can be used to overcome a specific issue that you have. Never should you feel that a mantra is forced upon you or that you feel obligated to try something as this goes against the tradition. Mantras, like Hinduism, are a way of life.

WHAT CAME FIRST; THE VEDAS OR THE MANTRAS

Both Vedas and mantras have been around for thousands of years. The Vedas are the teachings of Hinduism and are possibly the oldest religious works in the world. They are written in Sanskrit, a language with 3500 years of history. Many believe that even before writing, the Vedas were practised in profound meditative states until they were written down somewhere between 1500 and 500 BCE.

Veda- meaning knowledge

As language was far from developed, the Vedas focused on silence in order to gain knowledge of the energy pathways in the universe. Most specifically, yogis concentrated on vibrations and their patterns. When in silence, you are able to sense the universal vibrations. These vibrations led to sounds but no specific words, which became mantras. Each sound is a way of connecting with the divine and has specific healing abilities.

Mantra- meaning mind (man) and liberate (tra)

Words and meaning came later, as did translations and how we use modern mantras. Even words are made up of sound waves that create vibrations. Vac is a Vedic goddess and the mother of Vedas. She is the goddess of speech and the mother of Emotions. As human brain function began to develop along with language skills, it was Vac who enabled those she loved to put words to sounds and emotions.

The key takeaway is that the power of the mantras does not come from pen and paper. As soon as you start to write mantras down, whether sounds or words, they start to lose their quintessence. Unlike the Bible, Vedic mantras are written down so that the tradition can stay alive, not as a teaching tool.

As you can see, Hinduism stands out from many religions because there is no one belief. There isn't one God that you must follow but instead, a collection of powerful rituals

THE USE OF MANTRAS IN OTHER RELIGIONS

As Hinduism is the oldest religion in the world, there is no great surprise that younger religions and belief systems have borrowed aspects from it. The rosary of the Virgin Mary in Catholicism is a prayer bead, prayer beads have significance in Buddhism, and was probably borrowed from the Hindu prayers in India.

Mantras are no different. Chinese Buddhists include mantras in their spiritual practice but as their culture was more focused on the esteemed written language rather than the sounds, it became normal for Chines Buddhists to write mantras as their spiritual practice.

Sikhs use mantras to concentrate their mind on God and making sure God is an integral part of their daily lives. Jews repeat phrases from the Hebrew Bible in the form of song, and some Islamic communities chant the 99 Names of Allah.

The Hail Mary in Christianity is a mantra, a prayer that is repeated! With regards to mantras in the modern world, the Vietnamese War lead to a number of New Age groups that looked for a world of peace, leading to the modern mantra "make love, not war". Transcendental Mediation is another new age group that use simple mantras in their meditation.

Many of the modern mantras are not related to religion at all but they are still a crucial part of the person using them and lead that person to a better understanding of themselves. Whether you feel connected to a religion or not is obviously entirely up to you, and not the purpose of this book.

Each mantra calls on a distinct attribute associated with a deity. Deities in Eastern traditions can be gods, goddesses, a creator or a supreme being. There are the gods of fire, of animals, of light, of the weather, Mother Nature and the Furies. Knowing that mantras are not dependent on religious beliefs will help you in finding the right mantras. We will cover a range of mantras that are connected to deities but have deeper meanings than what you may see on the surface.

SO, WHAT EXACTLY IS A MANTRA

There may be no surprise here but coming from a religion where words are not the core of the lesson, there is no one definition of a mantra. Some will see words or sounds that allow oneself to free the mind. It can be described as the appreciation of sounds and vibrations in order to align your energies. Others use it as a form of prayer and some people who see mantras as a form of positive reinforcement through chanting.

Yogis will agree that a mantra is a blend of Sanskrit sounds that purify the mind, body and soul allowing the mind to experience peace in order to reach a higher self or Purusha. As this is a detailed subject, we will discuss it more a little later on.

The reason I like to start by going into the history and traditions of Hinduism is that mantras will generally only work when combined with the right understanding. Regardless of how determined you are, repeating a phrase is not enough.

It reminds me of when I was a kid and learning to dive. My father stood next to me and told me to say out loud over and over again "I can dive". If I said it loud enough, I would glide into the water with perfect elegance. The truth is, I belly-flopped. Telling myself (and embarrassingly half the pool) was only going to provide me with the confidence to dive, beforehand, I still needed to learn the stages of how to do a dive.

The words and length of a mantra will vary greatly. It is the purpose of the mantra that will remain consistent. We use mantras to declutter our mind from the trivial aspects of our daily lives. They will enable us to silence the buzz in our brains that occupy so much of our energy. Once your mind is quieter, you will be able to reach a state of self-awareness and empower yourself with the ability to make changes necessary. With that in mind, let's continue by understanding the three main types of mantras.

THE THREE TYPES OF MANTRAS

Before choosing a mantra or even a collection of mantras, you need to understand how each type has a certain purpose. One type has the power of healing, the other allows for spiritual development, and finally, a type of mantras that enable you to attain worldly desires.

Saguna mantras are used to personalize aspects or powers of God whereas Nirguna mantras are based on the principal truths of yogic philosophies and are not related to deities. Both are complex concepts to grasp and I didn't introduce these types of mantras into my routine until further on in my education.

I began with Bija mantras, the tradition of expanding the mind by using the power of vibrations. These mantras allow us to grow our physical, emotional, and spiritual side as if flourishing from seeds. Bija mantras are written in Sanskrit. The sounds are just one syllable and so are easy to pronounce yet have a great amount of power.

Bija- meaning seed

Here is where science kicked in and for me, the subject of mantras began to make a lot more sense in terms of logic. There are numerous studies and opinions regarding the Big Bang, again, nothing that we are going to debate. However, some believe that the universe was created by cosmic sound energy and light energy which created life. Cosmic sound energy, or vibrations, are directly related to life. By tapping into vibrations, we can connect with our energies and encourage balance within our mind and body.

For those who may need further convincing you only need to look at the benefits of psychoacoustics and the psychological responses to sound. Our bodies are made up of 60% water and as sound travels through water 5 times faster than through air the healing benefits of sound are immense.

If you take each syllable, or seed, from Bija mantras, you are able to combine them to form longer mantras. Imagine each sound as a letter of the Sanskrit alphabet. This is how the yogis developed mantras with certain purposes.

For us to be able to gain a sense of harmony, every part of our body must be in tune with each other. If you are experiencing mental or physical difficulties, it may well be because the rhythms associated with each body part is out of balance.

There are 7 Bija mantras that are used in yoga and meditation. When practising the following mantras, you can be lying down or sitting cross-legged, whichever position you feel comfortable in.

The 7 mantras are associated with a chakra, a spinning wheel of energy, and each one will control a different aspect of your life:

- **Root Chakra**- at the bottom of your spine, near the coccyx. It keeps us grounded and controls the things we need to survive, for example, money and food.
- **Sacral Chakra**- in the lower abdomen area. It

controls our creativity, sexuality, and can help us maintain control of our lives.

- **Solar Plexus Chakra**- found in the upper abdomen area. This chakra enables you to be yourself and be confident in doing so.
- **Heart Chakra**- slightly above your heart. It enables us to experience love, happiness, and inner peace.
- **Throat Chakra**- in our throat, or vocal cords. The throat chakra is essential for us to speak the truth and let others know how we feel.
- **Third-Eye Chakra**- located between the brows. The eye to our soul, it lets us connect with our instincts, wisdom, and helps us to see the bigger picture.
- **The Crown Chakra**- the highest part of our body, the top of the head. Its location is significant in spiritual connection and higher consciousness.

Chakras are fascinating and complex and while I want to briefly touch on them here and elsewhere in this book, book two in this series is dedicated to this wonderful subject and the healing benefits.

MEDITATION AND MANTRAS

You may have already discovered a type of meditation that suits you. I have tried various forms of the most popular forms and found positives and negative in each and it will be a personal preference. For me, I struggled with movement meditation, I felt that I was too easily distracted. It could be a very simple movement like rocking in a chair or going for a walk.

I fell in love with Mantra meditation because I was able to repeat mantras aloud, which helped me to focus more. Once I learnt how to control my focus better, I could repeat my mantras in my mind and take advantage of complete peace. I also felt that it provided a combination of benefits on top of my constantly wandering mind.

HOW CAN YOU USE MANTRA MEDITATION?

Mantra meditation is perfect for people who struggle to focus. When I felt like the world was on my shoulders, I couldn't see a solution that would relieve the pressure. Mantra meditation requires you to repeat a word or phrase. It is not the word that you need to focus on but the sounds that you create. When you think of a word our brain tends to start linking it to another and then another. You may have chosen the number 1, simple right. But when concentrating on one, you associated it with one thousand, then the money that you need to get your car fixed and stay on top of the bills.

Instead, concentrate on the sound of one, notice with vibrations of the first "w" sound, the openness of the "uh", the strength of "nu". Notice the difference in the sounds as you inhale and exhale, not forcing the emphasis of any of the sounds but letting them flow.

Repetition is crucial. Your mind will start to stray, and this is perfectly normal, but repeating your sounds, you will gradually regain your attention. A busy mind takes time to settle and you may find that takes a while before you start to feel inner peace. Even if it is difficult to slow the mind down, you will notice very quickly that it is harder for you to let negative thoughts into your mind when you are focusing on sounds. So, mantra meditation is a way to protect your mind from damaging emotions while you are mastering a deeper spiritual connection.

WILL MANTRA MEDITATION HELP ME PHYSICALLY?

Perhaps the reason you are reading this book is probably that you need help resolving your problems, either physical, mental, or a combination of both. Maybe you feel like your problems are under control, but you are looking for something more in life. A healthy mind is essential for a healthy body. Once you begin to focus your mind, you will begin to see what it is that you need in life. Mantra meditation brings about a positive sensation that will encourage you to make the necessary changes. It's not just used for finding a higher spirituality, it will give you the energy you need to improve your physical self.

Over the last few decades, more and more scientific research has been carried out on the physical benefits of mantra meditation. Results have shown that with the correct frequency of mantra sound, the brain can gain more oxygen, heart rate and blood pressure can be reduced, and brainwave activity is also calmer.

It is always necessary to practice mantras with a purpose and this applies to mantra meditation too. Before you begin, make sure you are aware of why you have chosen this type for spiritual growth. Is it because you want to improve your physical self? Do you need to quieten the mind? Or do you feel the need to create a stronger connection with the divine? Unfortunately, I often hear the answer "a little bit of everything" and although this is probably true for all of us, we need to tackle one aspect at a time.

BIJA MANTRA MEDITATION

Here are 7 very simple Bija mantras that can be used to improve the chakras that we covered before and some tips on how to pronounce them so that you get the right sound:

- **Root Chakra** – "Lam"- said as /lum/ like plum
- **Sacral Chakra** – "Vam" said as /vum/ like ovum
- **Solar Plexus Chakra** – "Rum" said just like the drink
- **Heart Chakra** – "Yam" said as /yum/ like yummy

- **Throat Chakra** – "Ham" said as /hum/ just like the sound
- **Third Eye Chakra** – "U" said as /u/ like the long sound in uber
- **Crown Chakra** – "Om" said as /aum/ as if you were feeding a toddler

Notice the major difference in the vowel sounds. The pronunciation of the mantras is deeper than how they are written as this comes back to the vibrations we emit when making sounds.

HOW CAN YOU USE THE MANTRAS IN THIS BOOK?

Hopefully, at this point, you have learnt some key concepts about mantras that will help answer this question. In the first place, I am not going to impose any mantra on you. The mantras you read in this book have been selected based on their traditions and teachings and how they can help certain issues you may have. You won't find a listicle of my top 10 favourites that transformed my life.

Different mantras should be repeated in different ways so that you can really benefit from them. Most are repeated 108 times. Why 108? The diameter of the Sun is approximately 108 times bigger than the diameter of Earth. The distance between the Earth and the Moon is around 108 times the diameter of the Moon. 108 sounds a lot but as most of the mantras in this book are short, it will only take around 10 to 15 minutes. Chakra mantras are repeated from the bottom to the top 1 to 3 times but can be for longer.

Read all of the mantras in the book, say them aloud, say them to yourself, concentrate on each sound. Decide if the mantra has meaning for you. If you need to write it down, it probably means that it doesn't have enough significance to become beneficial for you. The mantras that stick in your head are the ones that you should keep using. Those that don't light a spark inside you should be forgotten or keep them to one side in case a situation arises where they could become relevant. Use the mantras that feel right.

SACRED WORDS TO MANAGE
YOUR LIFE

This history lesson is complete but forgive me if I pop back to the subject here and there as I find it truly fascinating and I found great benefit in learning about how we came to today's mantras. Now, we are going to delve into the 4 main goals in life and which mantras will allow you to achieve them. Before that, I wanted to discuss the significance of mantras and our karma.

WHAT IS KARMA

Most people see it as "what goes around comes around", you laugh at someone who falls over only to go and fall over yourself. More so in the Western world, we wrongly associate Karma with bad luck or our destiny. In reality, it is just as possible for Karma to lead you to good things, if your actions merit it.

Like mantras, people use the word Karma in all walks of life regardless of religious or spiritual beliefs, but it is one of the principal concepts of Hinduism and Buddhism as well as other Eastern philosophies. It symbolises a life cycle that is dominated by cause and effect. One action you take now will impact your life later on. It's not limited to actions; Karma can be influenced by your words or even your thoughts.

Karma- meaning action

It's also worth noting that the intentions behind each action will determine the karmic result. A poor person who steals to feed their children is doing so out of necessity. Nevertheless, it is still stealing and will result in bad karma because it is morally wrong. Throwing a surprise party for your friend is a lovely idea, but if you are doing it for the recognition, your intentions are still wrong.

Mantras are mainly connected to yoga, meditation, and spiritual practises and this is a good place to start because you are in the right setting. But the ultimate goal is to practise mantras in our daily lives so that we can develop higher awareness and optimize our karma. As karma is a continuous cycle, we need to use mantras more frequently than our once a week yoga class.

There are four different types of karma. which are then defined in 148 subtypes. The four types are:

- **Sanchita karma**- the karma that has accumulated over all our previous lives.
- **Prarabdha karma**- the karma from our present birth. It cannot be changed as its built into who we are from birth.
- **Agami karma**- the karmic results from our willing actions. These actions impact our future karmic returns.
- **Kriyamana karma**- the more immediate results from our actions.

The subtypes range from higher to lower. Higher karmas are associated with the soul, knowledge and perception. Lower karmas include emotions, fear, anger, and false beliefs.

When we suffer from problems in our lives it's the lower karmas that take control. If we want to reach a higher place and start to enjoy life to its full potential, we need to remove the lower karmas and encourage the higher karmas. By adjusting our karmic patterns, we can start to move forward.

HOW CAN MANTRAS IMPACT KARMA?

Mantras will change our Agami karma. Mantras, as we now know, are a way for sounds and vibrations to reach our inner selves which then change our physical or spiritual self. Over time, a particular mantra will tweak our chakras and enable more positivity to flow through our bodies. The correct use of mantras allows higher karma to flourish while gradually reducing lower karma. With enough practise, we are able to eliminate the lower karma. One of the most powerful mantras is "Om mani padme hum".

Om Mani Padme Hum- meaning I prostrate to the Buddha Great Compassion/ Hail to the jewel in the Lotus

Om Bhrum Ayu Hum No Jah- meaning I prostrate to the Buddha Detached Lotus One

Om Ami Dhe Wa Hrih- meaning I prostrate to the Buddha Limitless Illumination

When combined, the three mantras are the ultimate way of destroying all negative karma. If you are still relatively new to using mantras, it might be worth starting with one and then building up to the mighty three. Even one of the mantras will start removing negativity and some believe that this can be carried on into future lives. It will open up your inner mind and help to reach a higher state of being.

MANTRAS FOR MENTAL WELL BEING

Like so many people, I felt like I was plagued by stress and problems and it was a huge upheaval just to try and organise my mind. I didn't want to try medication and I wasn't the type of person to discuss my problems with a specialist. My yoga instructor had briefly taught us how mantras would improve our physical and mental well-being, and this was enough to spark an interest for me to investigate further.

The 21st century has seen an abundance of studies connecting mantras to psychological well-being. One that caught my eye was from the University of West Virginia and involved Kirtan Kriya, a type of meditation. It is Sanskrit song that is used in conjunction with finger positions for each syllable in the mantra, Saa Taa Naa Maa.

Saa, Taa, Naa, Maa- meaning My true essence

Kirtan Kriya, when practised for 12 minutes a day over a 12-week period changed plasma blood levels and caused a biochemical transformation in the brain. This is because the vibrations created, along with the placement of the tongue, stimulated 84 acupuncture points that are found in the upper part of your mouth. Participants in the test experienced better cognitive function, a sounder sleep, improved mood. It also helped with reducing stress and higher levels of activity in the memory area of the brain.

As I read about the benefits of these 4 simple sounds, I felt as if they would lead to the help I needed to start overcoming my problems. I included Kirtan Kriya as part of my morning meditation ritual and soon noticed that the outside world was becoming less of a burden and although at first, the negative thought still rose up in my mind, I was better prepared to not let them affect me.

If you don't feel a connection with Kirtan Kriya, you could also try the following:

Om Gum Ganapatayei Namaha- meaning Salutations to the remover of obstacles

Om Shanti Om- meaning infinite peace

Bear in mind that though you will probably feel the psychological benefits fairly quickly, our problems, like karma, are a cycle so it is best to keep practicing your chosen mantra, even when you feel that your problems have been resolved. Our journey to higher self-awareness is a continuous one.

DEFINING OUR GOALS FOR A BETTER LIFE

The old saying, "you only have one life" is a bit of a contradiction when talking about Hinduism but for the sake of this part of the book, we are going to focus on the life we are leading at present. It's true that only with age do you start to appreciate the fact that we need to get the most out of this life. Time slips by and before we know it, we have sent a large portion of life doing what is expected of us rather than what we actually want. Generally speaking, our goals will change with time. Who didn't want to be rich when they were growing up? As adults, the goal might shift to 'financially stable'.

In Hindu teachings, there are four main goals according to Vedic tradition that can be found in the Upanishads. Collectively known as Purushartha and it is a concept that helps us determine our purpose in life and in order to achieve the four goals, excellent health is required.

Purushartha- meaning primaeval human being as the soul and original source of the universe (Purusha) and purpose (artha)

Arogya translates into 'without disease' and refers to the good health we require in order to go about our daily lives and for us to have a greater experience of life. A healthy lifestyle leads to a healthier body and mind. A healthy mind is necessary for the ability to think clearly about the goals we have in our life. For our physical health, we have to appreciate a zest for life and the energy we need to achieve our goals.

The main focus of this book is to reduce our ailments, and promote a healthier self all round, which is why the mantras are related to

Arogya. That being said, I want to provide some background into mantras for the four goals of Vedic tradition because you might find ties between the health and other goals, not limited to reduced stress when we are able to solve some of our financial issues.

WHAT ARE THE FOUR GOALS OF PURUSHARTHA?

Dharma- the goals related to our life purpose, they include our responsibilities, laws, and the proper way of living. The point of Dharma is to use the laws and structures in the world to reduce the chaos and remind yourself of who you truly are. It teaches you to be aware of your words, actions, and thoughts, highlighting the importance of karma.

Artha- related to material and financial prosperity and incorporates our career or how we earn our living. Artha incorporates human dignity and having sufficient material goods to enjoy a fruitful life but not to lead us to become greedy. Artha is about finding a career that both serves the community and makes you happy.

Kama- the pleasure acquired through non-material gain, our happiness, love, and the enjoyment of life. It's the beauty of life that we seek to find in art, literature and music. It is also the beauty we seek in relationships and intimacy. You might have associated the name with Kama Sutra, and while we can still experience pleasure from sex, the Kama Sutra is about experiencing sexual pleasure rather than a how-to guide.

Moksha- the freedom we seek to live and liberation from the cycle of death and rebirth so that we can reach our potential. By freeing yourself from life's illusion, you are able to gain self-knowledge and discipline and with this, you will appreciate a new level of realization.

Originally there were only Dharma, Artha, and Kama in the Vedic scriptures and in many ways entwined and one may depend on the other. Further on, Moksha was introduced as a way to balance the connection between the three earlier concepts. When you follow all of the values of the Purusharthas you will be able to access your current situation and make better decisions for your life.

HOW CAN THE PURUSHARTHAS BENEFIT YOUR LIFE?

Take a moment now to review your goals, and you must be honest. Don't adjust your goals so that they fit into one of the four goals mentioned above. This isn't a test to see if you pass or fail. Some people don't have clearly defined goals, or they assume that goals just to the grander aspects of life. Think about what you want to achieve or gain to make you happier.

We will use the example of 'Jessica' to put things into context.

Jessica is a 57-year-old teacher who wants to lose weight. She is completely stressed out at work because of senior staff telling her how to run a classroom. Her goals are to retire in 3 years and go to the gym three times a week, oh, and she wants to decorate her bedroom but has very little time to do it.

Jessica's goals are what she thinks will make her happy, and on a superficial level, they will. But there is no balance between the goals and so it will be difficult for her to improve herself as a whole. Once she has retired and decorated her bedroom, what will she be left with? Her job is one that contributes greatly to society, but it no longer makes her happy. A fresh coat of painting and some new sheets on the bed are certainly not too much to ask and won't make her greedy. She will appreciate the beauty of her room, but it's unlikely that this will aid her in discovering the beauty of the world.

For Jessica to find inner happiness and peace and to discover purpose in her life, she will need to reassess her goals in order to make sure they incorporate Dharma, Artha, Kama, Moksha, and of course Arogya for the mental and physical strength to bring to light all of her new goals.

Before you begin to practice mantras to accomplish your goals, you need to ensure that there are objectives for each of the 5 elements. Begin by writing the 5 words (Dharma, Artha, Kama, Moksha, and Arogya) on a piece of paper. See where your current goals fit and try to expand on them so that you have a balance of all five.

A MANTRA FOR EACH OF YOUR GOALS

Mantra masters encourage repeating a mantra 108 times between sunrise and sunset. Don't feel that you have to do this in one sitting. Some people will spread this out into two or three meditative sessions throughout the day. The most important thing is that your goals are clear and balanced and that the mantra you choose can be incorporated into your daily life.

Dharma

To discover your purpose in life, you first need to remove the obstacles that are blocking your path. Ganesh is the Hindu deity and the remover of obstacles. There is no coincidence that in some parts of India, Ganesh is married to Buddhi (intelligence) Siddhi (success), and Riddhi (prosperity).

Om Gum Shreem Maha Lakshmiyei Namaha- meaning pure force (Om), removal of obstacles (gum), the sound of abundance (shreem), increased energy (maha), lakshmiyei (life purpose), and completion (namaha)

Artha

For prosperity, there is a popular mantra that is actually a prayer to the earth goddess Vasundhara, the divine female or the bearer of treasure. It is also commonly known as the Buddha money mantra.

Om Vasudhare Svha- meaning Stream of treasure

While being blessed with prosperity and wealth, the ancient teachings were not designed for you to win the lottery. You should be blessed with enough to let you follow your spiritual goals without distractions from financial issues.

Kama

For increased pleasure as well as peace of mind and even reducing sins, this mantra has carious translations relating to the adoration of Lord Shiva.

Om Namah Shivaya- meaning O salutations to the
auspicious one

In Hinduism, Lord Shiva is one of the three most important gods. His role is to destroy the universe so that it can be recreated. He is also the patron of yogis and the protector of the Vedas.

Moksha

Becoming free and liberating yourself makes space for superior knowledge. This mantra isn't only about freedom, but it is also a message of how we treat others. It highlights karma and the fact that our thoughts, words, and actions should bring happiness into our lives and the lives of those who share our universe.

Lokah Samastah Sukhino Bhavantu- meaning May all
beings be free and happy

In Western philosophies, we probably use the phrase, treat others as you would want to be treated. You can see how the Moksha mantra can be used for more than one aspect of your goals.

AROGYA: MANTRAS FOR HEALING

When we talk about healing, we could mean a great number of different things. You might have the flu or a backache. You could be suffering from depression or addiction. Your healing might be for something obvious, or subtle, general or specific. So, when it comes to healing mantras, there are plenty.

Remember that the Chakra mantras we have been over are also used in healing. If you feel that you are lacking a sexual appetite, the "Yam" mantra will help to unblock your Sacral chakra allowing you to heal. With other healing mantras, you can use a specific sound that will correct the imbalance in that area, for example:

"Mmmmm"- the vibrations are directed towards the sinuses

"Nnnnnnn"- to alleviate problems with your ears

"Eeemmm"- for problems related to the eyes

"Gaa Gha" - to heal your throat

"Yaa Yu Yai" – this will help with any issues in the jaw

Alternatively, the five vowel sounds are non-local, which means you can choose one and mentally send the vibrations to the area of the body that requires healing. You will notice that although they are longer mantras for healing, most of them are Bija mantras, the seeds we need to replenish our health and align our energies.

Longer mantras do exist, even as long as 30 or more syllables and needless to say, to repeat it 108 times takes almost an hour. I discovered a healing mantra that ticked all of my boxes, and probably will for you too.

Om Ram Ramaya Namaha- meaning relieve pain, deep healing

This is actually a Rama mantra and the two syllables "ra" and "ma" are linked to the solar currents that flow down the left and right sides of our body (ra to the right and ma to the left. As they meet and cross at the chakras, these two currents improve your energies, a healing tool by itself. Ram is also the seed sound for the solar plexus chakra, which unlocks a large amount of dormant energy.

Another benefit of this healing mantra is that as a Rama mantra, it has great power in uncovering negative karma and eliminating it.

Without sounding like a broken record, these mantras are only ideas. If you hear a mantra that has a striking significance to your goal, then you should use it over the ones mentioned. Mantras are very personal and although many can be used for different purposes, it's the person who is using them that must understand the purpose.

As soon as I figured out my new set of goals and began using specific mantras, I noticed something that went beyond healing. My husband commented that I was more communicative, not about my day or what had happened with the kids, but about my feelings. Something that had probably been blocked before. It didn't mean that I was spreading my negativity, quite the opposite. I started to talk about the holidays we could take together, new restaurants we could try. It was when he mentioned this that I realized that I was beginning to see life from a different point of view. It wasn't a certain number of years that we had to try to survive, but instead a gift that we could use in any way we want to.

A MODERN TAKE ON MANTRAS

There is no doubt that as mantras have become more popular in Western cultures, they have been adapted and perhaps to an extent, modernized. There became a need for mantras in English.

English speakers are not arrogant about their language, and it's certainly not because we feel everybody should speak in English. Language experts have said that as the British are from an island, and historically haven't been exposed to languages like other countries have, they are somewhat shy about experimenting with new sounds and we definitely don't like making a fool out of ourselves.

We also live in a world where results are required almost instantly and not everyone has the time to learn about the philosophy behind a new concept. Personally, I found that using mantras in Sanskrit opened my eyes to the culture and I felt more connected to the traditions of Hinduism, Buddhism, and other Eastern philosophies that I learnt about.

Nevertheless, I appreciate that not everyone has the time to Google translate every Sanskrit mantra that they come across. Not only this, but there are also mantras that can't be directly translated or may have two translations with similar meanings.

HOW ARE ENGLISH AND SANSKRIT DIFFERENT?

You probably think I have lost the plot bringing up such an obvious question, but the answer is more about their purpose than what you see on paper.

English and Sanskrit were constructed for very different reasons. English is a tool for communication between others. We use it for directions, receiving information, and expressing emotions. Sanskrit was formed from a combination of syllables that were used to access a higher level of consciousness. As Sanskrit was being created, nobody was interested in asking the other for a cup of tea, their focus was communication at a higher level. In English, each word has a purpose. In Sanskrit, each sound has a purpose.

A lot of the mantras we have already seen are clear examples of how Sanskrit and English vary, particularly in sounds and syllables. Here is another of the most powerful mantras.

Nam Myōhō Renge Kyō – meaning Devotion to the Mystic Laws of the Lotus Sutra, or Glory to the Dharma of the Lotus Sutra.

Nam Myōhō Renge Kyō is a 5-syllable chant. The English equivalents have 14 and 12 syllables respectively.

How Are English and Sanskrit Similar?

One could argue that there are elements of Sanskrit in English. As the oldest language in the world, Sanskrit formed the basis of Latin, French, and German, all of which have contributed to English. The English language has very rich and complex vowel sounds. With 20 vowels sounds in total, it is one of the most intricate in the world. With such an extensive range of sounds, English is almost the logical language to choose over Sanskrit.

If you look at the following list of Sanskrit words and their English translations, you will see how there are clear links between the two.

Gau- cow
Matr- mother
Navagatha- navigation
Manu- man
Danta- dental
Naama- name
Maha- mega

That being said, a fat-free donut just isn't a donut, and while mantras in English can still have a profound impact, they will never be quite as powerful as those in the original Sanskrit. Let's take a look at how we can use the English language to gain personal empowerment.

HOW ARE AFFIRMATIONS DIFFERENT TO MANTRAS?

Affirmations are short expressions that have a powerful meaning to the speaker. By repeating an affirmation, you are able to tap into your conscious mind and alter your way of thinking and your behaviour. Affirmations are generally used along with positive mental imagery of the words you are saying.

"I think, therefore I am"

— *COINED BY RENÉ DESCARTES*

Descartes used this phrase as a way to prove his existence when others tried to convince him differently. Today this has become an affirmation used for a number of different reasons and can be adapted for any speaker. If you need to become more confident, you would repeat the words and imagine yourself full of self-esteem. When your brain hears it enough, it starts to act in this way. This affirmation can be used for people who want to improve their physical appearance, become stronger, more content, or more relaxed.

Approximately 80% of our daily thoughts are negative. When you think of our perspectives in this way, we could all benefit from choosing an affirmation.

The main difference between an affirmation and a mantra is that when using an affirmation, it is the words that provide power and energy, rather than the sounds and vibrations. Although that's not to say that the vibrations won't help.

HOW CAN YOU BENEFIT FROM AFFIRMATIONS?

In many ways, the benefits of affirmations are similar to those of mantras. They can be used to find motivation, whether that's for large or small activities. How many times have you got off the sofa saying "I can do this" as you look at the mountain of ironing? While providing you with energy for the woes of day to day life, they can also make you more active about personal development and the transformation of yourself and the world around you.

By activating a more positive brain, affirmations will help you to see the world differently. The person you have been putting off seeing all of a sudden doesn't appear to be that bad. In turn, communication becomes easier, even more enjoyable.

With the additional energy and motivation you discover from using affirmations, you will be able to tackle your goals with more gusto. Your goals become easier to achieve as concentration is elevated. As you become more open, you can meet new people and as your circle of friends grows, you benefit from more wisdom and more connections that will also help you to reach your goals.

When I first started to use affirmations, I was reminded of the infamous scene from the film, Jerry Maguire. This film left us with a legacy of affirmations, the most obvious being "Show me the Money". Tom Cruise begins stressed and unwilling to play the game uttering the words with a complete lack of spirit. Even Cuba Gooding Jr. claims that this is a very personal and important thing for him. As Cruise is forced to repeat the four words, he becomes louder, more convincing, and more determined, finally reaching his goal.

Relax, there is no need for you to shout your affirmations to the world unless of course, you want to. But I liked the scene because it was a clip that many of us can relate to from frustration to achievement with the help of simple words.

HOW TO USE AFFIRMATIONS IN YOUR DAILY LIFE

There are so many affirmations to choose from, some are longer, others shorter. Like mantras, it is important that you choose affirmations that ring true to you. Discover what you want to gain from your affirmation before you begin your search. Keep the ones you like, discard the ones you don't. Even if you start with an affirmation and you feel like it doesn't strike the right chord, don't be worried about changing it. Here are some ideas for inspiration:

- I love my job and the tasks I perform
- I am valued
- I am loving and lovable
- Life is full of love and I find it everywhere I go
- I love everything about my body
- Everything I think, say, and do makes me healthier
- I am enthusiastic about every second of my life
- I am beautiful
- I set myself free

If you feel that you have multiple areas that you need to work on, you can choose two or three affirmations to create a set, but again, make sure each one is specific to a certain area. If you are new to affirmations, stick to one to start with so that you can focus more easily.

Affirmations need to be repeated daily and with consistency, so it is important to try and incorporate them into your daily routine. It could be as you exercise, shower, drive to work, any time that you have 5 to 10 minutes without interruptions (so keep the mobile away from you).

It is always best to repeat your affirmations in two sessions, at least. I find the best time of the day for the first set is first thing in the morning as the first thing you tend to do is start thinking about your goals for that day and this way, you can begin with a positive mind.

The other time I like is just before going to bed. It was that time of the day when I used to struggle with anxiety, and this would lead to a sleepless night. If you repeat your affirmations before going to sleep, they become ingrained in your subconscious while your mind is resting.

Keep going for at least 30 days. By then, you will be comfortable with your words and will have found the best times to repeat them. At this point, they will have become as natural as brushing your teeth and easier to maintain in the long run.

AFFIRMATIONS TO STEER CLEAR OF

You have been talking to a few friends about how you want to use affirmations and naturally, they want to help and mention a few that they have heard. The first suggestion is "I will be happy". The problem here is that the affirmation is in the future, and your subconscious doesn't understand this.

Our subconscious works in the present and has no concept of the past or the future. Even if your goal is to be happy in the future, you need to use the present tense so that you subconscious understands that this is happening now. If you hear an affirmation that you like but is in the past or the future, keep the same vocabulary and change it into the present.

Another problem I have come across, and even to the untrained eye, it is illogical, but some people use negative affirmations. Unless your goal is to become weak, repeating the words "I am weak" is only going to reduce your strength. Choose affirmations that are positive, that make you smile, or make you feel warm inside. A good affirmation should make you feel like you can climb Everest.

HOW CAN YOU FIND THE RIGHT MANTRAS WHEN YOU DON'T HAVE A FAITH?

Not everyone believes in one god or many gods. Whether you believe that a man sits in heaven watching down on us, or that the gods are walking among us, or that there is nothing beyond what we experience in this life, there is a mantra for you.

There are even Buddhist teachers who recommend mantras for those who don't belong to any faith. Animals too have been known to heal from mantras. We can only assume that animals are not concentrating on the sounds of the mantra, which suggests that mantras will have a positive affect even for those who don't consciously believe in a higher being. This has further encouraged the use of mantras in the modern world.

Ironically, it is medicine's turn to catch up with ancient traditions. In the 60s, Hans Jenny conducted an experiment on how sound could create form in a number of substances. Images of water were taken before vibrations, 500 people sending positive thoughts, and prayer, and then again, after. The results were striking, and even scientists struggle to deny the impact.

As technology has advanced through the years, we now have the ability to witness tangible results of the mantras and meditation. MRI scans of before and after mantra meditation show a significant change in brain activity. The Gayatri Mantra produces 110,000 sound waves per second and scientists have concluded that it helps with tinnitus, Alzheimer's and Parkinsonism.

Om Bhur Bhuvah Swah
Tat-Savitur Vareñyam
Bhargo Devasya Dheemahi
Dhiyo Yonah Prachodayat

Here is a guide to the correct pronunciation:

/Om bhoor bhu-wah swa-ha
Tat savi-tur-varen-yam
Bhar-go-de-va-sya dheem-a-hi
Diyo yo nah para-cho-day-at/

The Gayatri mantra meaning "We meditate on the most adored Supreme Lord, the creator, whose effulgence illumines all realms. May this divine light illumine our intellect". While the

English translation has powerful religious vocabulary, the Sanskrit pronunciation has profound medical benefits.

I am trying not to influence your mantra decision in any way, but I do have one particular non-religious favourite people feel comfortable saying.

Lokah Samastah Sukhino Bhavantu- meaning May all beings everywhere be happy and free

The following two non-religious mantras can be used to instil confidence and self-belief or to liberate yourself from the mental or physical problems you are facing.

So Hum- meaning I am that

Om Gate Gate Para Gate Para Sam Gate Bodhi Swaha- meaning Gone, gone, way gone, beyond gone, awake, so be it

The ancient traditions of Hinduism are closing the gap between science and medicine and allowing people to improve their physical and mental health regardless of their stand in society, their age, gender, or beliefs.

DECIDING WHAT TO SAY WHEN YOU MEDITATE

We have touched on this before but it's an area to revisit because the more you read on, the more insight you will have into finding mantras that work for you. We know that mantras have to be for a specific purpose and used with focus. And we have reassessed our goals in life and chosen mantras that will help us to achieve them. It is also necessary that your mantras are in line with your personal and religious beliefs.

Many people start to feel overwhelmed when it comes to finding a mantra, like they are about to take an exam or that the rest of their life depends on it. Granted, your life will be greatly impacted but there is not a single mantra that is going to harm you. Deciding on the right words, you will enable yourself to feel a stronger connection to what is important in life.

To help you choose the right mantras, I have put together a list of related vocabulary for various mantra purposes. Each group is based on common issues we face or goals that we want to achieve. This is by no means a complete list but just another tool for inspiration.

Mental well-being - stable mindset/ emotional stability/inner balance/mental balance/ health of mind/ peace of mind/ mental soundness

Physical well-being- physical form/body state/ physical condition/ fitness/ physical status/ weight/ache/pain/ physical suffering

Career vocabulary- employer /employee/work/skill/ qualifications/ethics/values/ income/ salary/learning styles/ time management/promotion/ career ladder

Relationships- partner/ family/friend/love/ marriage/ communication/ ties/ loved ones/romance/kinship/bonds/matters of the heart/ commitment/faith/security

Tangible and non-tangible attainment- fulfilment/realization/winning/ acquirement/ completion/gain/ reap the efforts/reap the rewards

Higher state of being- higher power/ spirituality/subconscious/inner thoughts/ empowerment/acceptance/liberty/wisdom

Stress- anxiety/nerves/patience/lack of hope/depression/strain/worry/unease/irritation/sadness/guilt

These words should start you on your path to understanding what your mantra should be for. It should have the same effect as your favourite song, calming, motivational, inspiring and happy. It might be the words that you connect with or the beat but as soon as you hear it, you feel the benefits.

CREATING YOUR OWN MANTRA

Because what holds us back is often very individual, you might find you need your own mantra. You may have been searching for a while and found that the mantras are too specific, or not specific enough. Your mantra should represent the way you want to live your life, a sign of your values and ethics that are related to your goals.

Anything can be a mantra, a set of words, sounds, hums, so there is no reason for you not to blend your own words for the perfect, unique mantra. You may find you can combine words from the different lists if they work to achieve one purpose, for example, "I have the confidence to carry out my work". Notice that this is still a specific mantra with a motive.

Regardless of whether you choose Sanskrit or English mantras, you should focus on the individual sounds of each syllabus. Appreciate the vibrations and imagine the area of the body that is healing.

Mantras can't be distracting, which is why ideally, they are kept short. There should be no learning of a mantra as the words and sounds are supposed to be natural. Chanting your mantra aloud will help to centre your concentration. Chanting in silence brings forward a greater sense of peace. It's a personal preference and no right or wrong way.

A summary of what to remember when creating your mantra:

- They must ring true to you and be used for a specific purpose
- Mantras should be in line with your goals and your beliefs
- They should bring you peace, motivation, and happiness
- They should be short and contain either words or sounds
- They need to be in the present tense and positive
- You can be sitting or lying, chanting, or in silence, it's most important that you are comfortable
- Mantras will be most beneficial when you use them consistently and incorporate them into your daily life
- No mantra is dangerous, it's not a magic spell

When I created my own mantra, I decided I wanted a combination of the ancient and the modern. Sanskrit gave me a deeper connection with the philosophy and original teachings. At the same time, I had found a lovely English mantra that helped me to pull my attention to the present and appreciate just being.

"Om Shanti, I am here"

This was the first mantra I developed for myself. It was the starting place for my own journey. Using mantras before had most definitely helped me get out of the rut that I was in and feel more positive. It was true that I was beginning to appreciate the simple things in life like the warmth of the sun on my face. When my children started to argue I used to get frustrated and escalate the situation, now I just feel grateful that I have children as others can't. It wasn't until I started repeating my own mantra, I felt that instead of following other people's paths, I was creating my own and I needed this to discover my purpose in life.

THE SIGNIFICANCE OF LANGUAGE AND INTENTION WHEN USING MANTRAS

For me, it's quite upsetting that the language of Sanskrit is slowly becoming extinct. I have had the privilege of being able to travel quite a bit in my life and I find that exploring the less touristy areas really forces you to try and speak even a few words of the language. It provides a closer connection and appreciation of the culture. Going to China and ordering fried rice is no different than popping down to your local takeaway until you try saying *Chaofan.*

Travelling through India, Thailand, and Sri Lanka probably allowed me to learn more about mantras than I ever would from trying to learn by myself. Not because I took part in classes or had one-on-ones with yogis and Buddhas willing to share their wisdom, but because I had the opportunity to experience the language.

In 2011, it was estimated that Sanskrit was spoken by less than 1% of the Indian population and mostly used by Hindu priests. It is only the official language in one Indian state. This predominantly spoken language is losing its importance in a modern world that places English and other languages ahead.

Hearing this, I felt a sudden urge to learn at least some Sanskrit in a naïve attempt to spread the word and keep the language alive. In this chapter, I want to follow up on the importance of correct pronunciation of mantras so that the most can be gained from each one, so that you too can get a touch of the culture, and so that the strong traditions can continue to be passed on from person to person as they were intended to be.

It was my first trip that filled me with determination and enthusiasm, though I will confess, I soon reverted back to the shy student from school who couldn't pronounce a single word in French. I am going to assume that you aren't one of the less than 1% that speak Sanskrit, and it is quite possible that you will feel the same way as I did when learning how to pronounce mantras. The trick is to overcome your fear of getting it wrong. As with meditation and yoga, the Sanskrit pronunciation takes a little time to perfect.

WHY IS SANSKRIT PRONUNCIATION SO IMPORTANT?

We have already touched on this so now you know that if your yoga instructor is stringing together a bunch of sounds, there is actually great significance behind them. Each sound in a mantra will produce a vibration that leads to healing a certain area or help you to reach a particular goal. Our Chinese example of fried rice (*Chaofan*) in Cantonese is also slang for "have sex". The wrong pronunciation or even intention could lead you to get something you hadn't expected!

Sanskrit is a language of the gods, and this might put some people off from the start. It is necessary that we understand the translation so that we can select the right mantra, however, it is also important to remember that you aren't necessarily praying. Look at it like how some say, "Thank God". They aren't literally thanking God; they are expressing relief.

In a way, mantras are the same. If you want to connect with the gods, the best way is to use the oldest, divine language. On the other hand, each letter or bija is created by a sound, and it's the sound that we will focus on, rather than the words.

What I am trying to say, without offending the religious or the non-religious, is that though some of the most powerful mantras were originally prayers, they also serve another purpose. Whether you want to practice because of curiosity, spiritual enlightenment, healing, or just to escape from the turmoil of life, it's the sounds and vibrations that we are going to concentrate on.

SHOULD YOU CHANT MANTRAS?

There is no simple answer to this. I know from experience that in the beginning, you feel a bit of a fool, especially if you are practising as part of a group. I can also tell you that silent mantras encourage a greater sense of peace. Finally, I can reiterate that Hinduism encourages students to find their own path and so nobody will tell you whether you should or shouldn't chant.

While yogis and even advanced students are able to benefit from Nada yoga, it does require more concentration. Nada yoga uses the power of sound or the conscious use of sound. Instead of words, the person pays close attention to every sound they hear while meditating, from the sound of your breathing to a footstep in the distance. Nada yoga is about inner sound rather than the chant.

Nada- meaning Sound

Traditionally, mantras were meant to be spoken, some even sung with music. It is how they still remain so meaningful today in a language that is far from common. Your body and mind will be able to absorb the vibration without a conscious effort to direct the sounds.

Take the words "We will, We will, Rock You". Read them in your head as you would any other written sentence. Now read them aloud. Which feels more powerful? Which gives you more motivation or gives you a greater 'can do' attitude? Now hum the tune and focus on getting the exact pitch. Notice how even humming the right tune makes you feel better than simply saying the words in your mind. This is the reason that despite experience, I still chant mantras.

HOW TO PRONOUNCE SANSKRIT WORDS

If you have ever seen the International Phonetic alphabet (a little bit like Jolly Phonics in schools) you will know that each sound is represented by a symbol. The pronunciation of a word is between two forward slashes. When you translate a word online you have probably seen the forward slashes and symbols.

Vowels

In English, there are long vowel sounds and short vowel sounds, as with Sanskrit. The long vowel sounds have a colon after them. So, the word ship is represented as /ʃɪp/, with a short vowel sound. Whereas sheep is /ʃiːp/. In Sanskrit, the long vowel sound is represented with a macron above. The Sanskrit *i* is produced like the English *i* in bit. The Sanskrit *ī* is longer, as in the *i* in twice.

Diphthongs are blends of two vowel sounds. Here are some examples or Sanskrit diphthongs:

- e- /ei/ like in wait
- ai- /ai/ like in my
- o- /əʊ/ like in show
- au- /aʊ/ like in cow

Consonants

Retroflex sounds are consonant sounds that are made with the tip of the tongue rolled back towards the top palate and produces a deeper sound than in English. The position of the tongue in this way isn't used in English and it might take a while to get the hang of. Let's look at some words to help:

- d- /d/- like in dog
- n- /n/- like in never

Then there are what's known as the dental sounds. The tongue is very close to the front teeth and you may even detect a vibration that you wouldn't in English.

- t- /t/ like in team
- n- /n/- never

Notice that the t, n, and d can either be retroflex or dental and you can tell the difference with the Sanskrit symbols:

- त् - the dental t, ॒ – the retroflex t

Other sounds

When an r is followed by another consonant in Sanskrit, it is pronounced as /ri/. The first sound in the word Vrksansana would be said like /vrik/.

Sh and Sa are both pronounced in the same way (one less to remember), /sh/ like shoot or shut.

Va is pronounced the same way as we would in English, for example, vain, unless it is followed by another consonant it would sometimes be pronounced like a w. The Sanskrit word for master is svāmi and it could be pronounced as svami or swami.

Words that contain pha or bha are also pronounced in the same way and with an exhale on the p sound, imagine you are saying pathetic.

Luckily, there are also a good number of sounds that we would pronounce in the same way as in English, such as k, g, ch, and j, sky, chain, god and jump respectively. It is also worth bearing in mind that there will be different native pronunciation depending on regional dialects.

HOW IMPORTANT ARE THESE SOUNDS?

Very important! Just as they are in English. Sheet has a long vowel sound, but for a foreign speaker who pronounces it as a short sound, they may well make a bit of a social blunder. The

Sanskrit short *i* vowel is used to enhance energy, focused around the right eye, and encourages will power. The long *i* vowel is concentrated around the left eye and helps with emotions, creativity, and understanding. Once again, it goes back to the purpose of the mantra and each sound that is produced.

THE INTENTIONS OF MANTRAS

In Hinduism, all matter in the universe comes from Prakriti, a fundamental layer that provides us with three qualities of energy known as gunas and all three are constantly present in the living. Our energy, matter, and consciousness can be altered depending on our thoughts and actions.

Prakriti- meaning nature

Sattva, Rajas, and Tamas are the three gunas that we are able to control but we can never completely remove one. We can though, use yoga, meditation, and mantras to adjust the gunas and as a guide to achieving a better understanding of oneself and the universe.

Sattva is a state of harmony. It is the intelligence we are able to acquire and the pleasure we get in giving. Sattva is also associated with liberation, kindness, helpfulness, love, and a sense of balance. It's the gratitude we feel and the self-control we have.

We should intend to enhance our sattva as it will diminish the other gunas.

Rajas is a state of action and change. It's one that is easy to understand as it is what draws us to our careers but unfortunately, it is reaped with worry, stress, irritation and aggression and it is also linked to the chaos we have to try and survive.

Tamas is a state of inertia. It fills us with self-doubt and guilt, and it is what makes us ignorant. Laziness, boredom, addiction and apathy all arise from Tamas. When you feel like you are lacking energy, you are confused and hurt, it means that Tamas has too strong a hold on you.

It is easy to say that tomorrow I am going to wake up in a better mood. I will be more positive. We are hoping that Sattva will be more present. And while you don't literally cry over the spilt milk that didn't make it into the coffee, the first sign of a bad day and our good intentions disappear.

Mantras can be used for good and for bad. There are some people who will practice Tamasic mantras in order to manipulate others or even for destructive purposes. No, it's not black magic, but it does appeal to the dramatic side of some people. While negative energy may be projected onto others, it may also bounce straight back to you and increase your negative karma, so it is highly recommended not to practise these mantras.

Rajasic mantras are used for gaining status, money, career opportunities, in many ways they will feed the ego. You still need to be careful with these intentions as although your goal might be to improve your career, it is possible that there will be a negative impact on your karma.

With the help of Sattvic mantras, we can focus on the fundamental things we need in our lives, a roof over our heads, our family around us, freedom and good health. When you are choosing your mantras, always make sure that there is good intention behind them.

Sattvic Samkalpa- meaning Good Intention

Our use of mantras should not only be with good intentions for ourselves but also for others. Your spiritual path or the journey to your inner self will be more fruitful when you can help others along the way, and this will help with your good karma too.

Fun fact, to increase your sattva, it is worth trying to adjust your diet. Try to decrease your meat intake as well as processed foods, stimulants and spicy foods. Replace them with whole grains and fresh fruit and vegetables, when possible, those that are grown above ground.

Your lifestyle plays a crucial role in the balance of the gunas. Overworking and even taking part in excessive amounts of exercise and listing to loud music can increase your rajas while overeating, sleeping for too long and living in fear will increase the tamas, neither of which is what you should be aiming for.

HOW LONG SHOULD YOU USE MANTRAS FOR?

This is another question that doesn't have a simple answer. Most of the traditional mantras are repeated 108 times. The number 108 is a sacred number in Hinduism, not only for the distances in our solar system but also because there are 108 sacred sites in India, 108 Upanishads, and 108 scared places of the body (marma points). Japa refers to a type of meditation which requires the repetition of mantras a certain number of times.

In my early days, I felt it was impossible to keep count. It was like trying to count sheep while trying to sleep. I would get to the 30s and my mind would start to drift, debating whether I had missed one. That was when I was introduced to malas. A mala is a string of beads. Different malas have different numbers of beads, typically 108, 54 or 27. These beads are a tool that helps you to follow the number of times you have said your mantra without focusing on the actual number. You simply slide your finger over a bead.

Mala- meaning Garland or Wreath

A mala is very similar to a rosary in Christianity. Some historians believe that when the Romans explored India, they came across the words jap mala. As jap meant rose to the Romans, then mala became the rosarium and as English developed, rosary.

Like a rosary, the mala will have a head bead, known as the guru or meru. The guru bead can represent a higher power for some. For others, they see it as the greater connection to the universe. One common rule is that the guru bead is never counted, and therefore it is the 109th bead. The guru bead is rotated when the japa is complete, so the person knows to start the process again.

When I was travelling, I was tempted by beautiful beads and my eye would fall on the materials and colours that I liked. But needless to say, the material of which the beads are made of also have their own purpose and intention, I used this as the perfect excuse to start an amazing collection! Moonstone is a good material choice if you are looking to calm your emotions, onyx for self-confidence, and rose quartz helps to remove negative energy.

Colour can have an effect too. Purple represents spiritual values, yellow inspires creativity, and orange will help you to find more enthusiasm for things. Obviously, malas are going to be a huge benefit with helping you focus. My advice would be to have your intentions clear before finding out the best colour and material for your mala.

The other thing that will determine the length of time is how many mantras you have chosen, whether you want to use one mantra or a combination. Ideally, you should aim for 2 sessions a day of about 10 to 15 minutes, don't worry if it's less or more. But please make sure you are giving yourself enough time to complete the correct number of japas. Each repetition should be slow and calm, and you can't speed up towards the end as you see the hands on the clock spinning round.

PREPARING TO START YOUR MANTRAS

The time has finally arrived! You have reassessed your goals and you have a clear idea of your intentions. You have either selected a mantra that you feel a connection with, or you have created your own. Even if you haven't found the perfect mala, there will be time for this. A plain beaded mala will serve for the right purpose. Now it is time to begin.

Decide on the right location

Half of me would giggle while the other half was envious as I looked at some of the images of mums sat in the typical yoga position with kids running around, washing flying all over the place, but they have this perfect pose about them. Perhaps those closest to attaining enlightenment may succeed in this environment but I still find it impossible.

I need to know that the basic jobs in the house are done, at least those that you can see. Even if I'm in the living room and there are dirty dishes in the kitchen, I know I won't be able to focus.

I also find that it helps if I am alone. Not so much now because I feel more confident. But in the beginning, there was still something that made me feel a little silly chanting. I suppose it's no different to the first time you run a meeting or try a new sport. Being alone removed the distractions and allowed me to really feel a connection with the sounds I was making.

I have tried sitting on a chair, standing in the tree pose, sitting crossed-legged, walking, you name it, I have tried it. I still find sitting cross-legged to bring the best benefits. It's comfortable, it improves your posture, and it allows for deep breathing. Grab a few cushions for support under your knees or ankles if you prefer.

For me, the best place is my living room or the park as long as there aren't a lot of people around, only because I want the peace that those 15 minutes bring. There is enough hustle and bustle in our daily lives, and this should be time for just you.

Decide on when to start

Now this is an easy question. Today, now, tonight, tomorrow morning. There is no time like the present and you have the most important thing you need to start practising mantras - your mind. Cushions and malas will help, but if you don't have them, don't let that be an excuse not to start improving your life.

MANTRA PURUSHA AND THE BODY OF SOUND

It was so valuable for me to learn about the Sanskrit alphabet. I am by no means fluent but the mantras I use I can use to the greatest potential because I decided to take the time to perfect the sounds. Sanskrit is a beautiful language, one of the angels and gods. It is the only language in the world that transmits its meaning through sound and vibration rather than an emphasis on the meaning of the word.

At the same time, it provides incredible healing powers and not only for those with religious beliefs. The Hindi gods will not show their wrath if you use the power of Sanskrit for healing rather than to communicate with them. While our aim is to reach enlightenment, this can mean different things to different people.

I used to think that enlightenment was a mental state that allowed a level of spirituality that was closest to God. It was something that was almost unattainable, for not even the Dalila Lama was there yet. If he hadn't reached this spiritual bliss, then what was my hope!

Then I felt the need to decide what enlightenment meant to me. The word itself made me feel that it was about lightening my load. And this was one of my main intentions, not to palm my responsibilities off to other people but to mentally relieve some of the things that were weighing down on me.

Another of my intentions was to learn more about myself. Without sounding theatrical, I wanted to learn what my life was about, what I hoped to achieve from it, and what I was still capable of achieving, so enlightenment also became about self-realization. Because mantras don't require a religious belief, I appreciated that this was how I was going to improve my physical self and achieve my own definition of enlightenment. We have briefly talked about chakras and how each area has a mantra that will increase the energy flow into the spinning chakra. In this chapter, we are going to look at Mantra Purusha and the joining of the healing science of the mantras with marma therapy.

WHAT ARE MARMAS?

Ayurveda, or the science of life, defines marma as a medical term referring to the vital parts of the body. Marmas can be categorized as muscular, vascular, ligament, bone and joints and each one is located at junction points in the body, where two or more meet, for example, the wrist, neck, elbow, knees, even finger joints. When using mantras for marma therapy, you are able to alter frequencies in the body which can help remove negative thoughts from the mind and improve karma and sattvic qualities.

Marma- Meaning Vital parts

Imagine these marma points as bus stops and the passengers on the bus being the energy in your body. As the bus transports passengers around the town it drops people off and picks others up, connecting the town. The marmas in our body help connect the body, mind, and conscious. It joins the physical and the non-physical, the matter and the energy.

A marma is not the same as an acupuncture point. There are more than 400 acupuncture points and they are minute, holes in the skin that could allow energy to flow. A marma is an area that can be from an inch to approximately 4 inches in size.

THE THREE ENERGIES OF EACH MARMA

All of the 108 marmas in our bodies contain three energies or doshas, Vata, Pitta and Kapha. These biological energies inside the marma are what makes us individual in terms of our physic, mind, and emotions and if you consider yourself, you may see if and how your energies are not balanced and within Ayurveda medicine, Vata, Pitta, and Kapha are incredibly important.

Dosha – Meaning Fault or Disease

The doshas are derived from the five elements; space, air, water, fire, and earth. One of the three will be more apparent but at the same time, it is possible that you notice certain qualities from a second dosha, known as a dual-doshic constitution.

Those who have strong Vata energies have qualities that reflect the elements of space and air and will sometimes have dry skin. They usually have a slim physical appearance and fine bones. They are fast, both in the mind and with their actions. Pitta dominance will see a person who might have an oilier complexion, warm to touch, is quick to fly off the handle, and they have a fiery personality as their elements are fire and water. Finally, Kapha represents water and Earth. They are calm and often have a more solid body frame and may also have an oily complexion.

Our thoughts and actions play a role in the balance, increase or decrease of our doshas. They are also impacted by the food we eat and the physical activities we participate in. The ideal balance of the doshas is more often found in newborns, those who are still innocent to the negativity in the world and the attraction to the things we like that are no good for us. The more stress we find ourselves under, the greater the imbalance becomes.

During the time that I was learning about doshas I found myself thinking how awful I treated my body. This is not the road to go down, there is no point in feeling guilty for the bar of chocolate and the glass of wine you had last week. It does go to show, and it is worth remembering that how we treat our body has a huge effect on our physical and mental health. We already know this, the glass of wine may have given you a hangover and made you grumpy, however, I'm referring to a bigger picture.

While there are some things we can do to help encourage a balance of the doshas, exercise, relaxation, a balanced diet, etc., there are other things in today's world that are almost impossible to avoid. The stress of commuting to work, getting stuck in traffic, the constant buzzing of mobile phones with things that need to be handled straight away, money, the kids...it all builds up within us and it's only when you are on the brink of burnout that you realize the extent of the imbalance.

The phone isn't going to stop ringing and the traffic, unfortunately, isn't going to just disappear. So, this is where we can use

Mantra Purusha and the marmas in our body to begin to correct the imbalance of our doshas.

HOW ARE THE SANSKRIT SOUNDS RELATED TO MARMAS?

The Sanskrit alphabet reflects the prime powers of creation. Aside from our bones and organs, we have a life force energy called Kundalini. This energy sits at the base of our spine and as we become more awakened and our bodies are more in balance, this energy passes in an upward flow, almost activating each chakra until reaching our mind. For me, the unpoetic version of this is the game at the fairground where you have to swing a mallet so that a bell rings at the top. By using the sounds of Sanskrit, you are able to encourage the flow of Kundalini and heal parts of your body.

Kundali Shakti- meaning Serpent power

There are 50 sounds in total, each sound or seed has a specific location on the body. Before we go into the body parts, I wanted to explain more about how the mantras are created. There is a short mantra and a long mantra for each marma. The short mantra begins with Om (the source, or sacred sound), followed by the bija sound. The longer versions begin the same way, but they also include the word namah (salutations) and the part of the body. Let's use the first vowel sound as an example.

- Om Am- the short mantra
- Om Am Namah Sirasi- The vowel sound that relates to the head (sirasi)

You will notice that an *m* has been placed after the sound. This occurs with all of the sounds so that the bija becomes a mantra.

The 16 vowel sounds all relate to the head. I won't list them all, but I will include a few so that you get the idea. I will include the long mantra and you can decide which version you choose to use.

- Om Im Namah Daksina Netre – the right eye
- Om Ūm Namah Vāma Karne – the left ear
- Om Rm Namah Vāma Nāsapute- the left nostril
- Om Om Namah Adho Dantapanktau- the lower set of teeth

You can see how specific the marmas are. We aren't just saying that you can chant a mantra if you have a bit of a cold. There is a specific mantra that can alleviate congestion in the right nostril and another for congestion in the left nostril. In Western medicine, you would be given a nasal spray, if you haven't been told the usual "take paracetamol", which apparently fixes anything.

Moving onto the consonants. There are three groups, 10 for the arms, 10 for the legs, and 5 for the abdominal area.

- Om Kan Namah Daksina Bāhumūle – the right shoulder
- Om Nam Cam Namah Vāma Kūrpare – the left elbow
- Om Jham Namah Vāma Hastāngulyagre – the tips of the left fingers
- Om Tam Namah Daksina Pādamūle - the right leg
- On Dham Namah Daksina Pādāngulimūle – the root of the right toes
- Om Pam Namah Daksina Parsve- the right side of the abdominal area
- Om Bham Namah Nābhau- the navel

As well as picking up some anatomy vocabulary, you may have worked out the words for left and right too, which is something I struggle with even in English!

Finally, there are the semi-vowels and sibilants that focus on tissue, mind, and soul.

- Om Lam Māmsātmane Namah Kadudi- the soul of the muscles and the palate
- Om Van Medatmane Namah Vāmāmse- the soul of the fat tissue and the left side
- Om Sam Asthyātmane Namah Hrdayādi Daksahastantam- the soul of the nerve and the heart to the end of the left hand
- Om Sam Sukrātmane Namah Hrdayādi Daksa

Pādāntam- the soul of the reproductive tissue and the heart to the end of the right foot

Please don't confuse the mantra, the Sanskrit name of the body and the name of the marma. With all the new vocabulary it can be overwhelming, but nobody is expected to remember everything. It's unlikely that you will need to try and learn all of the Mantra Purusha. You only need to focus on the areas where you wish to see an improvement.

If you are determined to chant the long mantras that is great, but don't forget the traditional method of teaching and learning, through words and sounds not pen and paper. Luckily, we have so much technology that can help us with this, so my advice is to record the mantra on your phone so you can listen throughout the day and practice the pronunciation before you begin your japa.

HOW TO USE MANTRA PURUSHA FOR HEALING

Through meditation, we are able to develop a connection with our consciousness, our Purusha. Meditation lets us remove the negativity in our minds and the source of our pain. By using mediation and Purusha mantra, we can work towards healing both the mind and the body. It provides an opportunity for us to detach ourselves from the body which can then offer us some freedom from our pain.

It would be an insult to science to state that mantras will cure cancer or treat heart disease. Never should any reputable spiritualist recommend meditation and mantras as an alternative to the treatment that a person is receiving. What one should hope to achieve is some form of relief.

"Repetition of mantras is the best means for the alleviation of all diseases."

— *KARMATHA GURU*

The emphasis here is on the word alleviation. The best way to show you how healing with mantra Purusha is to tell you about a friend of mine and her experience.

Unlike my eccentric friend who we met at the beginning of the book; I have a friend who probed me about my learnings. She knew I had started using mantras and she was interested after seeing a difference in me. I wouldn't have called myself an expert at this point, but I had learnt enough to explain how our energies worked and which mantras could be used for different purposes. It took her a few more weeks to open up about her problem.

The poor thing had been trying to get pregnant for a couple of years and with no luck. Her and her partner had tried a round of

IVF and still she wasn't pregnant. She was due for her next round of IVF in 5 weeks and she was convinced it wasn't going to work. As she told me her story, I could feel her pain and although I had never used mantras to boost fertility, the mantras I was using were reaping wonderful rewards and I was convinced they could help her.

She was tied up in so many emotions, when she began talking it was like opening the washing machine door when it was still on full spin. I think even she was lost in so many feelings, most of which were guilt, anger, the envy of other mums, fear, and loss.

As she was open to the idea of meditation and mantras, I started to share my morning sessions with my friend. She learnt "Om Sam Sukrātmane", she chose to chant aloud and I marvelled at her bravery for a newbie. We sat side by side for 42 days, as she repeated her mantra and I created my own that I felt would help her.

Today, she has two boys and has said she has experienced more joy in these years as a mother than she had in all of her life before. She continues with her mantras, but now for other purposes.

My friend went through with her second IVF treatment. The mantras helped to alleviate her pressure, her tension, her negativity, and her conviction that the IVF wouldn't work. In our time together, my friend was able to learn that her goal wasn't to get pregnant. Instead, it was to be a good mum and to learn what unconditional love felt like. If you are a parent, you probably know that there is no other beauty in the world like your child smiling- a true beauty in the world.

During her mantras, it was hard for her to not think about the idea of being pregnant. It was a challenge for to take her mind off the idea of a baby and concentrate on the sounds and vibrations she was creating. It was a combination of the IVF and the alteration of her energies through mantras that made her a mum. Perhaps for those who are sceptical, mantras are a little bit like the divine; until you experience it, you can't appreciate it.

HEALING PARTS OF THE BODY

Mantra Purusha can be used to heal a great number of physical pains. If you want to relieve the pain in your lower back, you can work with "Om Bam". If you have had a car accident and you want to help the recovery process of a broken shoulder, there is "Om Kam". My eczema has completely cleared up since chanting "Om Yam", and I had tried multiple ointments, but still, I used them alongside the mantras.

HEALING THE MIND

Have you ever reached a point in your relationship where you have tried everything, but you can't find the words to get your point across? You blame them for not understanding, whether it's your parents, partner, or colleague. Can you remember the frustration of not being able to see the solution?

While each of the marmas has physical healing abilities, they can also have psychological benefits. Again, I'm not going to list all 50 of them, but some key marmas that will lead to mental healing.

- Am- feelings and expression
- Im- judgement and discrimination
- Um- listening and comprehension
- Rm- will power
- Dam- primary focus
- Dham- adaptation
- Nam- a higher mental connection

What happens if my right nostril is blocked but I don't want to increase my will power?

I'm not kidding, this was a question I was once asked, and I can see why! By now you have a good understanding of the intricacies of mantras and purpose. How one sound can lead to mental and/or physical healing. And the question really should highlight the importance of your intention. Mantra Purusha, along with all mantras, will have the most benefit when combined with intention. If your intention is to heal congestion in the right nostril, you need to focus your energies on this. On the other hand, if you want to increase your will power, then this is what your intention should be.

The Use of Mantra Purusha to Overcome the Pain of Our Past

There are some circumstances and experiences that no matter how hard we try; we can't seem to let things go. Even though decades had passed, the death of my grandfather haunted me. Childhood fears, though seem stupid to some, will still affect the lives of many adults. Despite wanting to move forward, there are things that happened in our past that we can't let go of, and until we do, the possibility of moving forward and creating a better life will be more difficult.

Our liver is said to hold unresolved anger. That family argument might be resolved in your mind, but your liver may still struggle to break down the fats you absorb. Similarly, the gall bladder holds on to feelings of hatred. If you feel like you can never get enough air, bear in mind that your lungs retain grief and sadness. Rather than our kidneys focusing on cleaning our blood, they also have to battle with our fears.

None of us actively seek to hold on to these emotions. More often than not, we assume that they have been dealt with until you hear a song, or somebody mentions a name and they all come flooding back. Even those who are healthy, strong, and in a good place in their lives can have a moment from their past that can metaphorically 'bite them on the bum'.

Learning how to use Mantra Purusha can help individuals recognize the pain they have suffered in their pasts and let go of this pain, even that which is subconscious.

As you can see, these seed mantras have immense power used individually or combined. By alleviating your physical and mental pains whether past or present. We all know how a toothache can be enough to stop you in your tracks, or backache can make it impossible to get out of bed, let alone make it to work. Learning about marmas and understanding your intentions can start the process of healing, clear away the negativity, and allow you some freedom from suffering. You will be able to clear the path so that you are ready to achieve your goals.

THE SOUND TO YOUR ENERGY CENTRES

While I wouldn't want to call one of my chapters 'heavy', I do understand that there was a lot of information in the previous chapter, lots of Sanskrit to pronounce and connections to parts of the body. We have learnt how crucial bija sounds are for certain healing purposes. This chapter will continue with the same theme but with a simpler set of mantras, the mono-syllable Shakti mantras.

Shakti- meaning To be able or Empowerment

Shakti is the personification of energy, the energy that is used in creation and change. Essentially, everything we see is energy, whether that is, for example, gravitational, matter or thermal. In Hinduism, Shakti is sometimes known as 'The Great Divine Mother'. As the primordial cosmic energy, Shakti has the power to be good, creative, and to heal, but she also has the power to do bad or create destruction.

Shakti mantras are widely considered to be some of the most significant and can be used in many ways; in yoga and meditation, for healing or energizing and more frequently in Hinduism, to worship the gods and to protect the different energies in the universe, the Shaktis.

WHAT ARE SHAKTI MANTRAS?

As mono-syllable mantras, they are words that contain vowels and consonants but only one sound, take for example cat, heat, knees, stretched, etc. In order to unlock the power of a Shakti, they must be repeated with incredible focus and an awareness of a power greater than we experience in our day-to-day lives. Though they are easier to chant, they can be more challenging to use because of the concentration required. For this reason, we are looking at them now rather than before learning about the importance of sounds, vibrations, and intentions.

There are ten primary Shakti mantras, each linked with a chakra. By practising Shakti mantras, one is able to begin the process of unblocking the energy wheels in our bodies. These mantras are:

- Om/ Aum
- Aīm

- Hrīm
- Shrīm
- Krīm
- Klīm
- Strīm
- Trīm
- Hum/ Hūm

I will discuss each one in much greater detail, but before, I wanted to go over the various applications of the Shakti mantras, so that you are aware of the uses and abilities.

THE VARIOUS USES OF SHAKTI MANTRAS

Deciding on the appropriate Shakti mantra will first depend on your goals, dharma, artha, kama, and moksha. Then, you need to consider the three gunas that will be used to provide the mantra with energy, sattva, rajas, and tamas. Finally, how you intend to use them, whether it's with yoga, Ayurveda, Vastu (the study of direction and balance), or Vedic astrology.

We will use Shrīm to see the different uses and just how the Shakti mantras are able to develop, maintain, and even diffuse the patterns and forces that we possess.

In terms of goals, Shrīm is used for the aid of financial gain and to advance our career and it connected with dharma and artha.

It will also assist with our kama goals by enabling us to achieve what we desire.

When looking at gunas, if you chose to use Shrīm with the intention of sattvic, you will encourage harmony and nourishment. With rajas, your aim will be to improve your outer self and accomplish more. Tasmic intention, the one not to be strengthened, has the ability to cause great destruction.

When used with yoga, Shrīm helps to fortify our devotion to the gods and guru. Ayurveda (the practice of medicine), one can benefit from healing. Vedic astrogeology ties Shrīm to the Moon and will help you to boost your strength. And finally, when used in Vastu, it is for increased happiness and wealth in the home.

It truly blows my mind all that can be achieved with one Shakti mantra. Now consider the applications of the nine other words and, at least for me, it's impossible to imagine not experiencing some form of healing when using them.

As we are focusing on healing and yoga, there is no need to burden yourself with all of the uses, but it just goes to show how one mono-syllable word can have such extensive capabilities. Again, it's when I look at the whole picture, I realise that although my eccentric friend may have been going the wrong way about it, her appreciation of the sounds was far more beneficial than either of us could have imagined at the time.

THE MEANING BEHIND THE SHAKTI MANTRAS

Om and Aum

TV, films, your yoga class, the chanting playing in the background of a holistic shop, it is likely that you have heard this sound prior to reading this book. Om is the prime mantra of the Purusha. It represents the essence of the ultimate reality, the universe. It enables us to connect with our true selves and the higher spirit. Om is the sound of the cosmic lord, Ishvara. He is an inner guru, a prime yoga teacher, and more importantly, the creator, preserver, and destroyer of the universe.

More often than not, you will hear Om chanted as Aum, the *A* signifies the creator and the waking, the *u* represents the preserver and a dream-like state, and the *m* calling to Shiva, the cosmic masculine force and a deep-sleep state.

Om helps us to clear our mind in preparation for other things, particularly meditation. Many of the mantras begin with Om as it is said that with a clear mind, the rest of the mantra will have a greater effect. Om allows our energy to grow and it takes the energy that sits at our spine and pulls it upwards passing through our chakras and flowing out of our body at the highest point. Aum will achieve the same thing but with a stronger force to move the energy up through our body.

In terms of healing and Ayurvedic medicine, Om encourages harmony within the body, the mind, and across the senses. Healing energy is drawn into the subconscious and overpowers our negative thoughts, even alleviating addictions.

Despite knowing how much power is associated with the vibrations produced with Om and Aum, some still find it hard to imagine the extent of its healing abilities. There are Upanishads and books dedicated to this sound alone.

Aīm

Pronounced /iaem/, Aīm is the feminine sound of Om and is the second most common bija mantra. The masculine and feminine sounds are often chanted together because this represents an understanding of all sounds.

Once our minds have been cleared after using Om, we are now prepared to centralize our mind and heart in a certain way. While we hear the sounds of Om, we visualize Aīm. As this mantra is the cosmic feminine force, there are plenty of mantras that are used for a greater connection with Shakti, the Divine Mother.

Aīm is also the seed mantra of the Goddess of knowledge and speech, Sarasvati. It will, therefore, help us to find the right words when we struggle to communicate. It is a wonderful sound to stimulate learning, the acquisition of wisdom and all kinds of knowledge but particularly to gain a better appreciation for the arts. It can also guide us in finding direction and motivation.

For healing, Aīm is still related to words, knowledge and speech. With concentration and awareness, Aīm can invigorate our vocal cords and allow our voice to be heard better.

Hrīm

The three sounds that make Hrīm are the Ha and Ra. *Ha* points to life forces, space and light while *Ra* has ties to fire, light, and dharma goals. *Ā* is the sound associated with energy, concentration and incentive. It is pronounced /hreem/ with a soft first sound and the tongue close to the top palate.

The use of Hrīm is more specific than Aim. As the prime mantra of the goddess and therefore the main Shakti mantra, Hrīm connects with the goddess across all of her principal powers; creation, preservation, and destruction. Its use is not limited to the goddess, but for spirituality, it can be used with any of the gods or even objects that we wish to bring closer to our hearts. It helps us to become humbler prior to receiving our hearts desires.

Hrīm is predominantly Pitta energy, it's fiery and intense but tamed down with a little air from Vata.

Speaking of the heart, Hrīm is the Shakti mantra for the heart. This means that it can help us with our emotions and feelings and to open up the heart chakra. It's that warm feeling when you see someone you love, the bliss you feel when you hear that person after a long absence, and overall, it is the Shakti mantra that allows us to experience joy.

For the physical heart or the actual organ, Hrīm can help to relieve the symptoms of heart disease and with the promotion of energies, it can increase blood circulation which brings about a number of health benefits including stronger lungs and an improved nervous system.

Shrīm

The Shrīm Shakti mantra is highly adventurous as it is the seed mantra of Lakshmi, the goddess of prosperity and abundance and it bears numerous blessings on her. She is also the wife of Lord Vishnu and provides him with his power and strength. Another name for Shrīm is Rama bija, worshipping Lord Rama, dharma personified.

Shrīm is pronounced /shreem/ with very little emphasis on the *m* sound. As the mantra of faith and devotion, it can be used to express your dedication to any of the deities as well as seek refugee with them. When used with religious intention, you may find yourself in favour with the deity to chant to. Like Hrīm, it relates to the heart but instead of the life force, it has more relation to one's feelings. The two can be used together, not just for the benefits to the heart but also because of the link between the Sun and the Moon, Hrīm being solar and Shrīm lunar.

Shrīm is primarily a Kapha mantra, the dosha of water and earth. It can be used to strengthen overall health, especially for women as it can improve the circulation to the reproductive system and enhancing fertility. It is a mantra to calm the mind but also has some pitta, a touch of fire to brighten our complexion. I have always wondered if this is what brings about the glow that appears early on in pregnancy.

Krīm

The first of the consonant Shakti mantras, those with an initial hard sound, Krīm is pronounced /kreem/. Broken down, there are three key sounds; *Ka* the presence of life force and the first stage of energy, *Ra* indicates the seed of fire and *Ā* as the concentration of power. This mantra produces light and intention, much like Hrīm and Shrīm, however Krīm is used for a more precise use involving a grander presence and stimulation of nature.

Kali is the goddess of time and change and the wife of Lord Shiva. Krīm is the seed mantra of Kali and with it, we can activate Kali's power. This power can in turn increase vibrations and give energy to everything. For this, we can see Krīm as the mantra of transformative energy, as well as the mantra of work and yoga.

Krīm calls upon the electrical energy that is present in the universe and it promotes action. Using Krīm allows us to take more control over our karma, both good and bad. When used internally, it arouses our serpent power (Kundalini). This results in greater perception, concentration and a deeper state of meditation.

When applied with Ayurveda intention, Krīm can produce a feeling of adrenaline as the sound is a fusion of Vata, wind and electrical energy, and Pitta, fire. While prompting action with the biological fires, the physical benefits may be noticed in the circulatory system and the nervous system, more so the heart and the liver.

Klīm

While Krīm is electrical, Klīm /kleem/ is its more feminine counterpart, the gentler side. If used correctly, Klīm can pull things towards us as if magnetized. Another quality is its ability to keep things in place, though if used with the wrong intention, Klīm may keep things down with power rather than choice.

As with many of the Shakti mantras, you can use Klīm to reach a deeper connection with any of the deities as it has a special relationship with Sundari, the goddess of love and beauty. It is also the seed mantra of desire and may help us to get what our heart honestly wishes for by reaching out to the deity that is able to help us attain our desires.

Klīm is the mantra of love, filling our hearts with this critical emotion. The benefits of Klīm are extensive and it is a popular mantra because it is so safe to use. As a watery Shakti mantra, and mostly Kapha, it is good for healing plasm and the skin. It can stimulate the digestive fluids and help us to absorb more nutrients. As a source of happiness, Klīm can have a calming effect, reducing nervousness and boosting the immune system.

Strīm

Along with the Ā vowel we have seen before, Strīm contains Sa, the sound of stability and Ta providing extension. Pronounced as /streem/ it has qualities of peace and as well as movement and the spreading of energy.

Some believe this is the Shanti bija, the seed of peace but it will also offer the power of the Devine feminine, aiding in childbirth, the ability to nourish and provide direction. Stim is rooted in the words stand, spread, take a step, and the elevate from one level to another and so our energy can extend horizontally or vertically.

With strong ties to the goddess of higher knowledge, we can connect with her or any of the deities to increase our energy for creative purposes. It can help us with poetry and art but also creativity with our language (not for telling lies), our ability to argue our point of view and debate.

Though not limited to women, for Ayurveda, it is a significant mantra for women's health, specifically helping with childbirth. With the right focus, you can experience both healing and empowerment, a stronger circulatory system and healthier bones.

Trīm

When you take away the *Sa* sound, you remove the element of stability and increases the *Ta* energies for horizontal and vertical expansion. Trīm, /treem/, when you highlight the Tri, you see the relationship with the number three and the bringing together of contrasts.

Trīm is the seed mantra of the Trishula, another connection to Tri. Trishula is the trident of Lord Shiva, his most powerful weapon that fights off evil and negativity. It is also believed to represent the three gunas.

This is an ideal mantra if you need help overcoming difficulties and harmful forces. The strong levels of pitta energy enable us to rise up into a higher state of awareness. The fieriness of pitta can also help us to feel braver, have the confidence we may need to be just a little more daring and take away some of the fear that prevents us from moving forward.

Hum

Said as /hoom/, Hum is another of the more important Shakti mantras next to Om and Aim. It is believed to be both the primal sound of Lord Shiva and the transformative character of the Divine Trinity.

Hum with a short vowel sound /hom/ is used when a person wants to relight fire, from the fire in our consciousness to the fire in our life force and breathing. It is good for removing negativity, burning it with lightning fire. As the seed sound of wrath, it can cause fiery energy too.

When pronounced with the long vowel, it can stimulate the ferocious manifestations of the goddess, like Kali and Chandi. On the other hand, its softer side is the seed of the sound of the Mother, with the ability to summon as well as avert.

Hum in its short and long vowel sound can uplift our Kundalini. It will kick our Tejas and Pitta into action, aiding everything from our digestive system up to our mind. In terms of Ayurveda, it can boost the immune system.

This is enough information for you to be able to use Shakti mantras in the right way, knowing how the energies will affect your body and mind. I love them all because they are easy to learn and to pronounce, so you really can turn your attention to the feelings that each one awakens and be more aware of the force each one produces. Needless to say, you can combine any of these mantras with other Sanskrit words and sounds to form longer mantras, but don't feel that this is essential.

HOW DO BLOCKED CHAKRAS IMPACT THE BODY AND MIND?

There are energy centres all over the universe, also known as a vortex, a swirl of energy. When these swirls are related to the body, they are called chakras. It's not like your pulse that you can feel beating, nor are they something you can see. What you will notice an improvement in your well-being when you start to unblock your chakras. There are 7 chakras that follow the path of your spine and each will reflect a certain quality in your life. In the first chapter, we concentrated on the location of the chakras, now let's see how they relate to areas in our life, starting from the bottom and working our way up.

Root Chakra

When your root chakra is blocked, you may find that you don't feel stable in life and that you lack security. It's normal for you to worry about the essentials in life like money, your home, food, etc. Physically, you may show problems with your legs, immune system and digestive system.

Sacral Chakra

This is linked to your creativity, your love for life and has deep ties with your sex life as well as your ability to enjoy yourself and have meaningful relationships with others. You may worry about being betrayed. Aside from affecting your sex life, you might have problems with the urinary system, lower back pain, and irritable bowel syndrome.

Solar Plexus Chakra

You will sense when this chakra is unblocked as you will have more self-control and self-acceptance. Your increased confidence will allow you to feel more optimistic. When blocked, you will worry about how you look and about being criticized

or even rejected. In terms of health, you might experience problems with your liver, stomach ulcers, high blood pressure and
chronic fatigue.

Heart Chakra

As one would assume, it has a profound connection with love
and relationships. When not balanced, this chakra can lead to
feelings of jealousy, a sense of being suffocated or a fear of being
alone. Heart problems may present along with pain in the
shoulders, arms and wrists. Asthma and allergies are also
common.

Throat Chakra

So close to the vocal cords, this chakra deals with communication, the ability to express yourself with self-esteem. You will
know how to let others know how you are feeling when the
throat chakra is unblocked. However, when blocked, you may
doubt your creativity. You may be susceptible to ear infections,
thyroid issues, sore throat and laryngitis.

Third Eye Chakra

When balanced, you will be able to enjoy clear thoughts, strong
instincts and more wisdom. You will be focused and determined. If your third eye chakra is blocked, or even unbalanced,
you might notice that you are moody, confused, and unable to
see things from another person's point of view. You could suffer

from headaches, blurred vision, a loss of hearing, and even hormone imbalances.

Crown Chakra

You will gain from a close connection to your inner self, you will be aware of your abilities and see the bigger picture. There are strong negative emotions when the crown chakra is blocked, such as anxiety, depression and a lack of power. Physically, you may be very sensitive to your environment, particularly light and sound and you might have dizzy spells.

It is not uncommon for people to have blocked or unbalanced chakras. We often put these symptoms down to the stress in our lives, or "I must go on a diet, start eating healthier". It's true, these things will help, but if we allowed ourselves to explore mantras to unblock our chakras, the benefits are almost unbelievable.

SHAKTI MANTRAS TO UNBLOCK YOUR CHAKRAS

Do not panic, there is not another list of mantras to decide from. The mantras are the same as the 7 bija mantras we have already seen. But the importance now, and where your intention lies, is in the Sanskrit sounds and seeds to open up your chakras. Now you will have a better understanding of how to pronounce them, so we will just quickly revisit them with a better understanding of their association:

- Root Chakra – "Lam"- opening up your survival instincts
- Sacral Chakra – "Vam" allowing you to feel more sensual and find your motivation
- Solar Plexus Chakra – "Rum" gaining more personal power, detaching from the ego
- Heart Chakra – "Yam" appreciating unconditional love
- Throat Chakra – "Ham" imagination and creativity
- Third Eye Chakra – "U" a stronger sense of wisdom, finding your inspiration
- Crown Chakra – "Om" the connection with the spirits and your inner self

As with some of the literal translations in Sanskrit, you may hear different mantras for the same chakra. For example, I have heard "U" and "Kshaam" for the third eye chakra. They will both achieve the same result, it's just a question of the regional dialect.

ARE THERE ANY ENGLISH MANTRAS I CAN USE TO UNBLOCK CHAKRAS?

Yes, there are. But remember that a mantra has to have meaning for you. I'm going to include an English version for each chakra, but you now have the knowledge to create your own mantras too. I wanted to give you a little challenge, not a test, but just to show you how much you have learnt so far. If you feel like it, cover up the names of the chakras, read the mantra, and see if you can associate the words with one of the chakras. To make it an actual challenge, the order isn't from the root of the spine to the head like before.

- **Heart Chakra** – "I am love, I give love, I am open to love."
- **Root Chakra** – "I am strong, supported, and abundant."
- **Solar Plexus Chakra** – "I am worthy of pursuing my passion and purpose."
- **Crown Chakra** – "I am one with the divine. I honour the divine within and around me."
- **Throat Chakra** – "I am in alignment with my truth. I speak with clarity and intention."
- **Third Eye Chakra** – "I am in connection with my spirit and I trust my intuition."
- **Sacral Chakra** – "I am the creator of my entire reality."

Even if you can't get them all, I'm sure you will be able to relate some of the English vocabulary with the appropriate chakra.

The Shakti mantras are the mighty sounds, the kiss that brightens your entire day, the complement that makes you feel sexy, the pat on the back from your boss, or the spare seat on the underground when you've had a long day. These are the

Hindu versions of the small things in life that make such a big difference.

I have said before that mantras can't be harmful, and this is still true. But these mighty sounds have mighty power and with the wrong intentions, they can cause harm. There is so much negativity and destruction in the world, there really is no sense in using the Shakti mantras to cause more. Not only this, but there is still a chance that Shakti mantras used with negative intentions will reflect back on you. Don't waste your time trying to seek revenge. With all my honest intentions, you have so much to gain when your chakras are unblocked and balanced, you will never want to waste your time with negative intentions. Healing is about you and let that be the focus of your intentions.

PART II

Part 1 of this book has been a rollercoaster ride of history, tradition, pronunciation and learning about the use of both Sanskrit and English mantras. We have dug deep into who we are and what you want to achieve from life and clearly defined our goals.

Though not discussing the religious aspects of mantras and healing too much, we have briefly discussed the great number of deities and how each one has its own mantra that will bring about certain benefits depending on the deity.

Throughout this section, we are going to look closer at key areas in which people feel they might need assistance, whether that's to heal emotions that they are suffering from, to discover new opportunities, or to relieve themselves from physical ailments.

You may find that I talk about certain deities in more detail here, but this is not because they are more religious or because you need to believe. It is simply because I love the history and tradition behind each mantra, and I feel that a greater understanding behind them allows for a closer connection to the sounds.

I understand if you want to skip straight to the mantras that lead you to a more fruitful life, the temptation to get started as soon as possible is strong. Don't forget to go through the others so that you are fully prepared for any ups and downs life may throw at you along your journey to a higher self.

BEFORE ALL HEALING; MANTRAS TO PREPARE YOURSELF

To an extent, you are have already made great progress with your preparation. You might have chosen some mantras and are putting them into practice but most importantly, you have discovered more about your true self. Not the person you feel you have to be for those around you or how you should be to fit into social settings. So, in this sense, you are prepared.

In this chapter, we are going to discover some of the ideal ways to prepare your mind. For the maximum benefits of a mantra, you need complete focus and concentration. This is a struggle when there is so much for us to contemplate in life. Whether you are employed, self-employed, working from home or retired, each of us has stress and problems and I know just how heavy a head we all lay on our pillows at the end of each day.

Now is the time to start clearing some of this emotional clutter. Before we look to achieve our goals and start healing physically, it is crucial that we prepare our mind and our emotions and lift ourselves out of the fog and into clarity.

With the help of one of my first healing groups, we are going to practice some mantras that will allow you to appreciate living in the moment, heighten your concentration, and discover harmony in your life and within yourself.

My first group wasn't really a professional group. I had begun an online community and there were a few ladies in my city that had shown an interest. It was simply a coincidence that we were all female and has no reflection on the use of these mantras. Looking back, perhaps my first website was a little feminine but we all live and learn.

Anyway, I loved my first group. Really at that stage, I was more of the organizer than the expert but being able to share the knowledge I had gained filled me with hope and confidence and I started to see my goals coming to light. We were also a very mixed bunch, so we were able to explore a range of mantras.

A SHANTI MANTRA FOR FINDING INNER PEACE

Jane was the youngest member of our group. She had been a single mum for a few years and now has toddler twins with her new partner. It was impossible for her to get any sense of peace

and it was hard for her to keep being the glue in what sometimes felt like two families living under one roof. There were
jealous tantrums and not only from the children!

We began with the simple form of the peace mantra, Om
Shantih Shantih Shantih Om because Jane felt was overwhelmed by the full mantra. After just a couple of weeks, she
was into the full swing of it and the long version had become
part of her morning ritual.

It is recommended to chant this mantra first thing in the
morning. As the twins were up (and fortunately going back to
sleep again) at 6.30 am, Jane changed her morning routine and
when the boys were back asleep, she chanted the longer
version.

Om Dyau Shanti-Rantariksha-Gwan Shantih
Prithvi Shanti-Rapah Shanti-Roshadhayah Shantih I
Vanas-Patayah Shanti-Viswed Devah Shanti-Brahma
Shantih
Sarvag-Wan Shantih Shanti-Reva Shantih Sa Ma
Shanti-Redi
Om Shantih Shantih Shantih Om II

May there be peace in the whole sky and in the whole
external, vast space
May there be peace on earth, in water, in herbs, trees and
creepers

May there be peace in the entire universe. May peace be in the Supreme Being Brahman
Also, may there consistently exist in all peace and peace alone
Om, peace, peace, peace to us and all creatures

After just one month, Jane looked like a new person. The grey circles under her eyes had faded and you could see a fresh sparkle. She felt that the slow repetition of this Shanti mantra enabled her to concentrate on the word peace and its meaning to her. She felt that as her mind became calmer, so did her home.

THE MOTHER OF THE UNIVERSE TO HELP US CONCENTRATE

Susan was all over the place and I mean this is the nicest possible way. She entertained the group with her numerous stories and often appeared to start another one before finishing the last. She had a teenage daughter who needed a lot of help with her studies and felt that rather than just concentration on the particular topic they were studying, Susan needed more focus on her life in general as she didn't know how to compartmentalize.

The Durga Mantras are used to worship Goddess Durga, who is also known as Shakti or Devi. As the protector of the universe, Maa Durga is incredibly powerful and can help protect us from negativity. As a mother, she shows great love but also has the ability to lose her temper.

Susan wanted to be more like Goddess Durga. She wanted to eliminate the negativity that was coming from her daughter and find the ability to focus on the different parts of her life.

Sensibly, she chose a relatively short mantra to help her remain focused, the Maa Durga Dhyan Mantra.

Om Jataa Jut Samaayuktamardhendu Krit Lakshman
Lochanyatra Sanyuktam Padmendu Sadya Shan Naam

I bow to the Supreme Power and urge you to help me
concentrate on my goals
And thus, help me to achieve them.

As I have said before, mantras aren't magic spells, and this didn't transform her daughter into a straight-A student. It helped Susan to focus on her work, then her daughter's studies, then her hobby instead of getting flustered by doing everything at once. The time she spent with her daughter was dedicated to studying and they both saw the positive results.

TUESDAYS FOR ELIMINATING OBSTACLES

Sophie was a sweetie. She worked in customer services for a supermarket chain and though she had tried some mantras but didn't feel like they were having the right impact. From talking to her, I got the feeling that the challenges she faced in her daily life were blocking her mind and that it was important to remove these obstacles before she could see the other mantras take effect.

Lord Ganesha is the magnificent deity whose head is an elephant's head. In Hinduism, many of the Gods have a day dedicated to them and Lord Ganesha's day is Tuesday. This isn't to say that you shouldn't chant it every day, but some will also choose to fast as well as pray to Lord Ganesha on a Tuesday.

Vakratunda Mahakaya Suryakoti Samaprabha
Nivighnam Kuru Me Deva Sarva-Kaaryeshu Sarvada

O Lord, with a curved trunk and a huge body, you emit the
radiance of crores of Suns
Remove all obstacles and bless me so that I succeed in the task
that I undertake now, and in the future
Crores- Indian, meaning ten million

This was a favourite for the whole group as it wasn't often in our Western culture that we were able to celebrate the larger body and gave us a chance to forgive the little extra weight we were carrying.

Sophie was able to handle her challenges at work so that when she came home, she wasn't plagued by the stress of work. She chose to chant this mantra the full 108 times in the morning and evening and on Tuesdays, she repeated the japa a second time, as she said, "just in case he is listening".

A TASTE OF REALITY TO APPRECIATE THE PRESENT MOMENT

Emma was a bit lost in life. She was caught up in her past and regretted a lot of her decisions. At the same time, she was putting an awful lot of pressure on her future and where she was heading. She too had tried some mantras but hadn't realized the importance of using them in the present tense.

It's something that we can probably all relate to. Even now I can still find myself carried away with the stress of the day that I feel guilty taking 5 minutes to just sit down and have a coffee and to use that time to be grateful for today.

Satchitānanda can be broken down into three words that also help with the pronunciation. Sat means being, chit means consciousness, and ānanda means bliss. As a mantra, it relates to the ultimate reality and can help you to pull your focus to the here and now. It was first mentioned in the Brihadranyaka Upanishad, one of the earliest Hindu texts.

Satchitānanda- meaning Reality consciousness bliss

Representing the absolute reality, some say this concept is the same as God, others say it's an experience beyond enlightenment that only a small group of masters have been able to achieve.

I felt that using this compound word, Emma would be able to start enjoying her life in the present so that she could gain some strength and perspective. Emma repeated Satchitānanda in the morning and evening but also during the day when she felt her mind would drift back to her past or future. It particularly helped to prepare her mind for mantras that she would then use to heal that which was bothering her from her past.

The four of us were nothing but dedicated to our progress. There was no such thing as group WhatsApp chats in those days (I say with a youthful smile) so the times that we got together were full of positive recollections of the week that had passed, where we had seen the benefits and what we wanted to continue to work on.

I suggested that we practised two mantras together as I wanted to get a sense of the power of the group while not in a yoga class. Plus, I thought that both of the following mantras we suitable for all of us.

THE LIGHT OF THE SUN TO BEGIN OUR HEALING

In one way or another, we were all suffering and we would all benefit from more positivity and warmth. While being lifted into the light of the sun, I also wanted to begin to heal our bodies and our minds.

The Hindu god of the sun is the Surya Devta. The sun is essential for life and growth and by worshipping Surya Devta, you will be able to gain from his light. As the god of the sun, it is best to start this mantra on a Sunday and then continue as part of your mantra routine.

Namah Suryaya Shantaya Sarvaroga Nivaarine
Ayu Rarogya Maisvairyam Dehi Devah Jagatpate
Oh Lord Surya, you govern the universe and treasure peace.
You remove all kinds of diseases. Bless me with long life, good health, wealth and prosperity.

My aim for this mantra was to go from removing negativity and then replacing it with positivity, or if we weren't to get there straight away, to at least be able to experience a bit more of a balance. To appreciate that by taking a wrong turn and getting lost at least led you to find a new restaurant you would like to try, instead of getting lost and the entire day ending up being a disaster.

In my mind, this mantra would create the feeling of when you are on holiday and you wake up on the beach with the sunlight on your face.

LOOKING PAST OUR SHORTCOMINGS

We were making progress, but I still felt that the ladies were too hard on themselves. There were physical aspects that we all wanted to improve however by giving into these flaws we weren't appreciating the true beauty of ourselves, and that was what was inside of us. My hope was to get these ladies to see their inner beauty just as much as their outer beauty.

For this, I went back to the Lord Ganesha mantras, after all, this god was plump and had the head of an elephant, yet looking at him, you just see a belly full of joy and we can all gain from his good spirits.

Om Sumukhaya Namah- the constant beauty in soul, spirit, in face, in everything

Again, I wasn't expecting us to meet a week later and to be filled with confidence about our perfect bodies and beautiful souls. But as with more balance between the positivity and negativity, I was hoping that to start with, every negative the ladies came up with, they were able to think of a positive. This, for me, would be a sign of progress.

We practised the new mantras morning and evening and once a week together for 15 minutes. What I also loved about our group was the freedom to practise our mantra in a way that we felt comfortable. Even when we were in a group, some sat, some lay down. It was very easy for us to get into the rhythm of the sounds, and it wasn't necessary for all of us to be chanting together. In fact, there were some weeks when we were all in silence.

And the thing that amazed me even more, was the energy that I felt as we repeated our mantras. This energy followed me, and I could even sense it when I was at home repeating them alone. It wasn't an energy that I had taken from the others and therefore was depriving them. When we discussed this feeling, the other ladies agreed.

The other feeling that we shared was that although these were chants to worship some of the most important deities in Hinduism, we still didn't feel like it was the same as sitting in church and praying to God. We respected the religion but perhaps because our focus was on the Sanskrit and the sounds, the mantras felt like a chant rather than a prayer.

This was a very important matter for me. In the beginning, I felt like I was taking advantage of the Hindu traditions. I imagined the deities watching over me thinking, "look at this cheeky one using our language but not praying to us". Learning more and more about these rich Eastern philosophies, I know this is not the case as they are traditions based on passing on wisdom.

And this is what our group did. We took steps to clear our mind in preparation for the next stages of our journeys. We did so with respect and a genuine passion for what we were doing. We shared what we learnt and saw the benefits of these powerful mantras.

On a personal note, I found that working with this fantastic group of ladies emphasized that I was now on the right path in my life. I had discovered that thanks to mantras, I was able to help people. Now it was time for me to step out of this comfort zone and find some men to join in my groups!

MANTRAS FOR EMOTIONAL HEALING

After the success of my first little group, I was on cloud nine. My learning had allowed me to really identify what areas of my life I wanted to change, and I could see the commitment starting to reap its rewards. Physically, I felt stronger. I was motivated to start swimming and the freshness of the water along with my heart pumping that little bit faster felt like I was cleansing myself.

I felt as if my family respected my role as a housewife more. Having more things that I wanted to achieve forced them to contribute and I no longer felt like I was the maid picking up after them. I didn't just leave them to fend for themselves, but it no longer defined who I was.

Another benefit I saw was my social life. For the first time since I think my teenage years, I had friends who were my friends, not Emily or Joshua's mum, not Simon's wife, but Verda's friends. Meeting new people gave me the opportunity to talk about my passion and I was pleased with the positive response to mantras and spiritualism. At first, I thought they were just polite responses. But when my new friends came back with questions, I felt like people really did acknowledge my expertise on the subject.

Nerves overcame me as I began to prepare for my next project, nevertheless, I knew in my heart that it was important to push forward, and I continued to alter the use of my mantras for the situations I was facing.

I decided it was time to promote my service. I didn't want people thinking that I was in this for the money, and so as not to turn my passion into something commercial, I chose to set up a donation system where instead of a payment, people could choose from one of three charities to donate to. This was a great way for me to help others in need and I also hoped it would reflect on my karma.

The next group I wanted to create was dedicated to emotional healing. Again, as a new project, I had no expectation but was delighted when the phone started to ring. I was even more delighted when I answered a call from a man! A few more male callers and I could tell that they were all still a little hesitant, so this led me to start a separate group for those who preferred a male-only environment. Those that were having doubts then came around to the idea. Perhaps it was one thing to try this rather "out there" idea but another would be to share their feelings with women they didn't know. Either way, I had 4 men who wanted to meet on a weekly basis to gain a better understanding of their feelings, and I ran another group alongside this which was predominantly females. I want to share with you want we discovered.

A MANTRA TO WELCOME CHANGE AND NEW THINGS

I could see that there were some people who were still sceptical, and I could understand this. It made sense, and amused my group, that we should start with a mantra for being open to change and to try new things. After all, if they were not willing to try, it would be challenging to see the benefits of other mantras.

I felt the need for an English mantra and a shorter, simple Sanskrit mantra that wasn't specific to one of the deities, something that the whole group could benefit from. Our English mantra was "I am stepping into the unknown. I am welcoming change".

This was a powerful mantra and it was easy to control our breathing, inhaling on the first sentence and exhaling on the second. For our Sanskrit mantra, we began with one word, repeated twice and pronounced as it was read.

Neti Neti- meaning Not this, not this

We used this mantra to accept the fact that there were things in our lives that we wanted to change. This was an excellent place to start because we learnt the importance of focusing on the sounds and vibrations rather than the actual 'this' that we wanted to change. The group felt that it was important to appreciate the need for change before working on ways to make them happen.

OVERCOMING OUR BIGGEST EMOTIONAL FEAR

We began one session talking about our fears. The most common came up, not being able to care for the family, becoming ill, one person said heights while another said birds. It wasn't until David (not his real name) admitted to fearing death that the others all agreed. This is a fear that can wake people up with a jolt in the middle of the night or it can alter the way they live their lives because they fear the consequences.

If you are able to overcome your fear of death, you will probably be able to overcome your fear of flying, as the fear of flying normally comes from the fear of a plane accident and death.

Lord Shiva has a thousand names, 1,008 to be precise. But it is the Lord of death and destruction that we require. Many misinterpret the "angry god" but his power enables him to destroy negativity as well as death. After the destruction, we experience creation and so Lord Shiva is also worshipped for his reproductive power. The mantra is called the Maha Mrityunjaya mantra.

Aum Trayambakam Yajaamahe Sungandhim
Pushtivardhanam Urvaarukamive Bandhanaat

We worship the three-eyed One who is fragrant and who nourishes all beings; may He liberate me from my death, for the sale of immortality, even as the cucumber is severed from its bondage of the creeper.

I was a little dubious about delving straight into the gods so early on. I chose to ask the group if they were interested in learning about the meaning behind the mantra and I was pleasantly surprised when they said yes, reaffirming that Hindu traditions are meant to be shared, not forced upon others.

Sometimes, to overcome our fears, we just need a better understanding of the situation. So, I followed up with one of the Vishnu mantras, which are widely used to overcome fears.

Om Shri Vishnave Cha Vidmahe Vasudevaya Dhimahi
Tanno Vishnuh Prachodayat

Om, let me meditate on Lord Vishnu, Oh Lord Vasudeva,
give me higher intellect,
And Lord Vishnu illuminate my mind

I didn't feel that the group was quite ready to learn about our healing energies just yet, and so we went on with mantras that we could all appreciate.

THE WIRING OF A MAN'S BRAIN AND A WOMAN'S BRAIN AND COPING WITH STRESS

Years ago, I watched the most hilarious video about how men and women have different ways to cope with stress. The Nothing Box from Mark Gungor was an amusing way to generalize how our brains differ. Again, generally speaking, men have just as much stress as women do, but they handle it differently. For example, a man might not feel comfortable discussing the emotions that arise when they are stressed. For this reason, I went onto a mantra that is intended to be used to handle stress and deal with negativity in the hope that it would open up the minds of this group to make them more aware of their feelings, instead of going to the metaphorical 'nothing box'.

Om Gajakarnakaya Namah

Salutations to the one who has the ears of an elephant

Though it seems quite vague, it actually means that as Lord Ganesha had the head of an elephant, he was able to hear a lot, but like him, you should only choose to use the positive things so that negativity doesn't cause further stress.

Regardless of gender, there are more ways that someone can suffer than just stress. So together, we also worked on the Devi Stuti mantra, another for the worship of Maa Durga.

Ya Devi Sarva Bhuteshu, Shanti Rupena Sangsthita
Ya Devi Sarva Bhuteshu, Shakti Rupena Sangsthita
Ya Devi Sarva Bhuteshu, Matri Rupena Sangsthita
Yaa Devi Sarva Bhuteshu, Buddhi Rupena Sangsthita
Namastasyai, Namastasyai, Namastasyai, Namo Namaha

The goddess who is omnipresent as the personification of the universal mother
The goddess who is omnipresent as the embodiment of the power
The goddess who is omnipresent as the symbol of peace
Oh. Goddess who resides everywhere in all living beings as intelligence and beauty.
I bow to her, I bow to her, I bow to her again and again.

As well as blocking out negativity, this mantra builds inner strength and helps people to create more meaningful relationships with those they love.

The weeks went by and the males in the group did start to open up more. They were more aware of the actions throughout the day that led to stress and with this, they were able to find the best times of the day to chant the mantra. Some found it was useful after lunch to help them during the afternoon while another mentioned the benefits of chanting before meetings.

LETTING GO OF THE GUILT YOU FEEL

Shaun had had a life of wrong decisions and a few situations that he wished he could reverse. As he had grown out of his 20s, he had come a long way in improving his life, but his past still haunted him. He felt a lot of guilt about what he had put his family through and noticed that this was still having an effect on their relationship today.

The feeling of guilt was one that so many people felt. The most common, and especially for the women in the group was the guilt of not being there for their children because they had to work.

The problem with guilt is that regardless of whether it is something in our past or in our present, the emotion eats away at us and prevents us from enjoying the great things we have in our lives.

Om Vishwani Deva Savitar Duritani Parasuva
Yad Bhadram Tanna Asuva

Oh Lord! The Creator of the Universe, remove all forms of vice and sorrow from us.
Give us those qualities that are ennobling

I loved how this mantra helped Shaun to let go of his past and get rid of his huge sense of guilt. On top of that, he began to live life with more dignity, he seemed to hold his head a little higher than in our first meeting.

ONE MAN'S FIGHT AGAINST LONELINESS AND DEPRESSION

Richard's divorce was finalized a year before our meetings, but the pain was still quite real for him. He was unable to move forward with creating a new life and though at the time he struggled to admit it, he was depressed.

One of the Buddhist concepts is that essentially, we are never alone, and we all connected to everything. When a plant converts carbon dioxide into oxygen, we all breathe the oxygen. This way, we are connected to the plants, animals, and other people and therefore, never alone.

Richard would benefit from a mantra from the Isha Upanishad that focuses on learning more about yourself. It emphasizes the idea that we are not alone.

Purnam Adah Purnam Idam
Purnat Purnam Udachyate
Purnasya Purnam Adaya
Purnam Evavashishyate

That is whole. This is whole
The whole arises from the whole
Having taken the whole from the whole,
Only whole remains

I also suggested that David practised the Green Tara Mantra. Green Tara is considered to be the Mother of all Buddhas and is associated with enlightened activity and prosperity. When worshipping Green Tara, we are asking for freedom from our sadness, for the mental strain that prevents us from experiencing freedom.

Om Tare Tuttare Ture Soha

I prostrate to the Liberator, Mother of all the victorious ones

Interestingly, when asked for advice with regards to the Coronavirus crisis, His Holiness the Dalai Lama suggested that chanting the Green Tara mantra could be helpful.

DISCOVERING INNER PEACE AND A CONNECTION TO THE WORLD

From each group, there was a person that shared the same traits. Paul and Denisa both bit their nails and they both had one leg that constantly shook. There was a nervousness about them, and I could get a sense that neither of them felt grounded.

In times like this, nervous chaos needs to be removed so that a person is able to gain more control over their lives. Lord Brahma is the creator of all life forms, time, and dimensions. The Brahma mantra is ideal if a person needs to combat inner and outer conflicts that arise.

Both Paul and Denisa were determined to make the changes they needed to make and didn't shy away when I told them that the Brahma mantra needed to be repeated 108 times before sunrise.

Om Eim Hrīm Shrīm Klīm Sauh Satchid Ekam Brahma

This is one of the more difficult mantras to translate. You will recognize some of the seed sounds that we have already covered, then there are 4 words that can be translated separately:

- Sat- truth
- Chid- the spiritual mind
- Ekan- one, without a second
- Brahm- the entire universe

While essentially worshipping Lord Brahma, Paul and Denisa also had to pay close attention to the seed sounds and the vibrations that they created.

The Brahma mantra requires long-term commitment and to see the true results, you need to practice for a year. That's not to say that we didn't see improvements. Watching them chant this mantra, I could see the physical symptoms of their nerves slowing down, the speed of the leg shaking slowed down and they were calmer in their conversations. It was amazing to see the same effects in two different groups.

THE TIME TO INTRODUCE HEALING ENERGIES

The atmosphere in both of the groups was optimistic. Nobody had questioned or doubted the power of the mantras we had been using, on the contrary, everyone was hungry to learn more. I felt it was the right time to introduce how our energies had the ability to heal both the mind and the body.

As I began explaining the benefits of Kundalini yoga, everybody eagerly sat in the right position. Now for many mantras, it is more important that you are comfortable and focus on the sounds. In Kundalini yoga, our goal is to activate the energy that sits at the bottom of the spine, so the person's position is as important as the sounds.

Ra Ma Da Sa Sa Say So hung

Sun, Moon, Earth, Infinity, all that is in infinity, I am thee

This is the Siri Gaitri mantra and is used when you are sat down, your elbows are close to your rib cage, and your forearms are at a 90° angle to your body with the palms facing up.

Along with the right position, it is necessary to be sat upright and to breath slowly, creating a visual image of the energy moving up through your body.

The opportunity to work with men and woman provided fascinating outcomes, I had seen that mantras were not limited to age, beliefs, or culture, and neither to gender. The use of mantras showed us that we were all human and that even though we express our emotions differently depending on our personal problems, there are solutions that will help any type of person.

Both the men and the women felt a sense of relief after a few months of using mantras daily. It was almost like they had a clean slate and were ready to move on to the next stage. They had discovered their emotional triggers and developed their own mantras to master their unique triggers. Those around them felt a greater sense of stability with fewer emotional outbursts. The men and women of the group had begun their journey to a more peaceful life.

MANTRAS AND RELATIONSHIPS

One of the first things people ask me when we start talking about mantras is if there is a mantra to find Mr. or Mrs. Right. A wise woman once told me that you have to kiss a lot of frogs to find your prince or princess. I have to remind people that mantras aren't a quick fix to find solutions, but they are a tool that will help us to achieve what we desire in life.

Those who have had their heart broken feel like it is impossible to find love again. Some people feel like they will never have sex again, a desperate thought in itself! The mantras in this chapter are going to help us to discover love. If you have been in a relationship for a long time, you might feel that you need to rediscover the love for your partner. This is perfectly normal, especially if you are unhappy with other aspects of your life. And yes, we will look at ways to recapture the lust we felt in the honeymoon phase and look at mantras that will help us to increase our sexual energy and to increase our confidence when exploring our sexuality.

At the same time, it is important to remember that relationships are not limited to our romantic partner. They can be with family, friends, co-workers and each type of relationship is susceptible to ups and downs, miscommunications and challenges. Before we investigate mantras for romantic relationships, I wanted to talk about how we can enhance all of our relationships.

OVERCOMING OBSTACLES IN OUR RELATIONSHIPS

I didn't have obstacles with my daughter in her teenage years; she was the obstacle. Obviously, I didn't want to remove her from my life, but I certainly needed help overcoming the problems we were having. The colleague at work who never refills the coffee pot, the mother who fusses, the friend who belittles you in public, I'm sure you can relate with your own personal experiences. I think it is impossible to go through life without some problems in relationships.

Om Vighnanashaya Namah- meaning Obstacles (vighna)
and One who removes (nashnay)

I really like using this mantra and teaching it to everyone who is looking to improve their relationships. For me, I found it was a good place to start, to remove the problems that I was having with people so that I was then ready to work on making a difference. It goes back to having a clean slate or a fresh canvas to work with.

UNDERSTANDING YOURSELF BEFORE TRYING TO FIX RELATIONSHIPS

My husband and I went through a "phase" where things were more than just rocky. It seemed that he could never see things from my point of view and that I was always the one making concessions. Reading a book on relationships might provide you with the knowledge, but it's only with experience in relationships that you gain wisdom.

Wisdom enables better communication and with better communication, you are able to get your point across without having to become angry or irritated. It isn't about backing down or proving that you are right. It is about learning to walk in other people's shoes. The Ganesha Gayatri mantra will help you improve your modesty and righteousness, as well as providing you with the wisdom to deal with other people.

Aum Ekadantaya Viddhamahe
Vakratundaya Dhimahi
Tanno Danti Prachodayat

We pray to the one with the single-tusked elephant tooth who
is omnipresent.
We meditate upon and pray for the greater intellect of the
Lord with the curved, elephant-shaped trunk.
We bow before the one with the single-tusked elephant tooth
to illuminate our minds with wisdom"

I often use this mantra to show people that it isn't always easier
to say the English translation! Lord Ganesha has one broken
tusk which symbolizes the importance of having more faith
than intelligence. I also find that by visualizing Lord Ganesha
while chanting this mantra, I am reminded of his large ears (to
listen more) and small mouth (to talk less).

GETTING IN TOUCH WITH YOUR VARIOUS SIDES

There is no scientific research or psychological study behind
this theory. It's just how I like to view myself and the idea helps
me get a better sense of myself as one whole being.

I find that I have a masculine side and a feminine side in the
traditional sense of the words. I love tearing down walls, fixing
the fridge when it breaks and taking care of my own car mainte-
nance. The downside to my sometimes-dominating masculine
side is that I am stubborn and won't ask for help.

On the other hand. I love to cook cupcakes with sprinkles and little hearts, I like painting my nails, and I can't resist crying at almost anything on TV. The downside, I am not good at talking about how I feel, and I am infuriated when my husband goes into his nothing box (if you can remember from the last chapter).

This is why I was over the moon when I came across three mantras that I felt would help me create a balance between the masculine and feminine side and allow me to appreciate a deeper sense of myself.

Om Aim Hreem Shreem -to call upon the divine feminine

This mantra is a combination of bija sounds Aim, Hrīm and Klīm, the female deities and feminine forces of the universe, Maha Saraswathi, Maha Lakshmi and Maha Kali, respectively. It is best to use a mala for this mantra at both dusk and dawn.

Hare Krishna- to call upon the divine masculine

Lord Krishna is a compassionate God who can help eliminate the struggles in our lives as well as allowing us an abundance of positivity and luxury. The time of day is not as relevant as the time you spend on this chant. You should repeat it until you start to feel completely relaxed and happy, this will be at least 108 times.

Om Namah Shivayah- to call upon the deity of all deities

Lord Shiva, the supreme deity responsible for creation, preservation and destruction. This is the perfect mantra to become at one with your inner self and to take your inner self to a higher level. You can practise this mantra throughout the day whenever you feel the need but try to make them part of your morning and evening routine in order to appreciate the deepest connection with yourself.

I have shared my theory and these three mantras with plenty of groups in the past and we all noticed that life no longer felt like Lego bricks that we were trying to stick together. When our masculine and feminine energies were not in battle with each other but rather in harmony, the various aspects of our lives fit together better.

Now we will turn our attention more to romantic relationships, but that doesn't mean that with the right intention, they can't be used for other partnerships.

WHEN YOU ARE LOOKING FOR LOVE

Traditional advice when we can't find a partner is that we are not looking in the right place, or we are going after the wrong type of person, we need to make a bit more effort, or we need a little patience. None of it really helps but the advice offers us a glimmer of hope for our love life.

A more productive approach would be to use a mantra to allow yourself to love. Instead of looking to change the circumstances, you can change yourself. More often than not, when you have had bad experiences in the past, we build a wall up around ourselves as a form of protection. It is a subconscious act; our heart wants to love but our mind is cautious.

Om Lambodaraya Namah- meaning Salutations to the God who has a big belly

Lord Ganesha has 21 names; the one with the beautiful face, the one who bestows success, the destroyer of obstacles. Repeating this mantra can break down your wall of protection, or your obstacle and it can allow you to see your true beauty. Just as Lord Ganesha loves his food, you too will be able to feel love again.

It is far more sensible to start with this mantra before you begin your quest for love. Similar to when we prepare ourselves before moving onto emotional healing, you need to prepare yourself for love. It can take 30 days to see the full benefits of a mantra. It is possible that you will see improvements earlier on but there is no rush. This experience should be exciting and enjoyable, not just, let's get it over with.

THE BUZZ AND BUTTERFLIES OF A NEW ROMANCE

Why on earth would you need a mantra now when this is the best part. You are at the stage when you are discovering things about each other, you are laughing at each other's jokes, meeting friends and family. Life is good at this point. Your new romance makes the working day easier; you sleep with a smile, and you exercise with vigour.

It is also a massive learning curve and not everything you learn you may like. When I saw this mantra that I am about to share, I immediately remembered the relationship between Hindu teachers and students. One that is built on offering wisdom rather than forcing it on someone. It reminded me of when my husband cooked something and kept saying "try it, just try it" (it felt like 108 times!) rather than offering a taste.

Om Sahana Vavatu
Saha Nau Bhunaktu
Saha Viiryam Karavaavahai
Tejasvi Nau Adhitam Astu
Maa Vidvissaavahai
Om Shanti Shanti Shanti

Om, may the Divine protect both teacher and student
Let us be nourished and protected
May we work together with great energy

May our studies be effective
May we never hate or fight one another
Om Peace, Peace, Peace

Sometimes in a relationship, you will play the role of the teacher and other times the student. Whichever role you are playing at the time, it should be with love and joy and without conflict. While this mantra was traditionally used for students and teachers, I felt a deep connection with the words and those first stages of a new relationship.

AWAKENING YOUR SEXUAL ENERGY

If you are blushing at the mere thought, I strongly recommend this mantra! I hate to generalize, and I am not a feminist, but in most Western cultures, it is still seen as "unladylike" for a woman to talk about sex. Society still doesn't see that women have primal needs just as much as men do. The "I have a headache" joke is just far too outdated for the 21st century.

It is time for woman and men to get more in touch with their sexual energy and to enjoy sex. Each person in the relationship should feel comfortable exploring their sexual energy and instigating sex when they want to.

To awaken our sexual energy, we need to go back to the Sanskrit sounds and seed mantras that open our chakras.

Sat Nam- meaning- I am truth

Because it is used in Kundalini yoga, it is important that you are sat in the correct position with your elbows tucked in and your forearms facing forward with your palms up. To really impulse the energy that is at the base of your spine up to your head, the Sat sound should be 35 times longer than the Nam and for at least 3 minutes a day.

HOLDING BACK THE GREEN-EYED MONSTER

Without wanting to talk about me too much, my husband called me jealous once after a night out drinking. He assumed that I was jealous because he had been socializing with other women, and this is a very common emotion to experience. However, what he couldn't see was that I was jealous that he had been out, talking to adults rather than at home cleaning up after the kids and following the usual mundane routine.

Jealousy presents itself for so many reasons. Many men I have spoken to become jealous of their wives when there is sudden career advancement, or even of the bond mothers have with their children. What is worse, is that nobody enjoys feeling this way, so it is necessary to alleviate yourself from possessiveness and jealousy.

Such a powerful emotion requires a powerful mantra.

Om Mani Padme Hum- Hail the Jewel in the Lotus

When used with the intention to overcome jealousy, I like to break the sounds down and see them as a story or a journey along a path.

- *Om-* bringing harmony and aligns energy
- *Ma-* taking away your physical needs and opens the door to spirituality
- *Ni-* freeing you from your desires, replacing them with peace
- *Pad-* liberating you from ignorance and bias so that love remains
- *Me-* letting go of possessiveness and learning to accept
- *Hum-* releasing the hatred within you

Tibetan Buddhists use this to reach the highest state of compassion and this popular mantra can be used for so many reasons. Don't forget the importance of intention and your personal goals when you chant this.

WHEN YOUR MOUTH IS WORKING FASTER THAN YOUR BRAIN

In the heat of the moment, we say things that we don't mean. Even before the other person has had a chance to react, we know that we shouldn't have said it. We have seen the mantra Neti Neti in the section where we wanted to change. Perhaps it is a situation you want to change or quash the words you wish you hadn't said, "not this, not this" is a wonderful way to stimulate change.

On a similar note, there will be times where you have to recognize that you made a mistake and while you need to ask for forgiveness from your partner, you may find help by using a mantra. This particular mantra produces immense power through vibrations which help to protect you from negativity or evil. It is also a little longer, so I practise the sounds and pronunciation with people before we begin to chant. You may want to save a video of the Shiv Dhyan mantra so that you can listen a few times.

Karcharankritan Vaa Kaayjam Vaa
Shravannayanjam Vaa Maansam Vaa Paradham
Vihitam Vihita, Vaa Sarv Metat Kshamasva Jay Jay
Karunaabdhe Shree Mahadev Shambho

Supreme One to cleanse the body, mind, and soul of all the
stress, rejection, failure, depression, and other negative forces
that one faces.

If you have ever made a health juice in order to detox, this is like an equivalent in terms of mantras. Many people I work with feel a sense of relief after a time practising this mantra and it helps to find forgiveness from Lord Shiva for the mistakes we have made.

LETTING GO AND MOVING ON AFTER A BREAKUP

You don't wish it on anyone but at the same time, a breakup is almost a rite of passage, a memorable experience that leads onto the next stage of our lives. We often compare it to the five stages of grieving or a series of emotions that need to be processed; clinging onto the past will only delay the process, speeding it up may unnaturally force it.

Whether the relationship has been for 2 months or 20 years, during that time, you will have created a bond that is difficult to just break. You will need time and space to discover how you overcome the pain and suffering you feel when a relationship ends. There are so many factors to consider, it is wrong to say it is time to chant a mantra and move on.

Because each breakup is different, I think it is important for people to create a mantra of their own to help them through suffering. You could be feeling sad, desperate, lonely, angry, bitter, or even guilty because you feel relieved.

In conjunction with your own mantra, I recommend the Purana mantra on Vishnu.

Om Apavitrah Pavitro Vaa Sarva-Avasthaam Gato-
[A]pi Vaa
Yah Smaret-Punnddariikaakssam Sa Baahya-Abhyantarah
Shucih

Om, if one is impure or pure, or even in all other conditions,
He who remembers Pundarikaksha, he becomes pure
outwardly as well as inwardly

Pundarikaksha- meaning Lotus-like eyes

Be careful of people who say that this is a mantra to bring love back. If a relationship is over, there is a good reason for it. Thinking that love will come back is a form of clinging to the past. This mantra allows us to free ourselves from the sins we have made but also to free ourselves from the ties that keep us locked to our past.

Relationships are a tricky business that we can often take for granted. We assume that once we have one it is set for life. But we forget that as we move through life, we change. The things that once seemed important are now replaced with more important goals. If your new goals aren't aligned with your partner's (whose will also change over time), then you will soon discover that you are on different paths.

In some cases, the goals are too different to come to an agreement and the best solution for both is to part ways. That being said, if you are able to start using mantras from the very beginning of your search for love, you may well discover that you are more open to love and the love you receive from others, you can enjoy a fruitful sex life for longer than the honeymoon phase, and you can learn to grow together, accomplishing individual and common goals.

MANTRAS FOR PHYSICAL HEALING

Which came first, the chicken or the egg? Was it your chronic headaches that led to your depression because you couldn't do what you loved in life, or the depression that weighed so heavy on you that couldn't shift the pain in your head?

Reliving our physical aches and pains will help us when it comes to emotional healing just like you may have already seen your physical self improving after dedicating time to your emotional healing. The body and the mind may be two different things, but they are living in the same vessel.

The last chapter of this journey will look at specific mantras that can help reduce the symptoms of illnesses and diseases.

I have said it before but is so crucial that I will repeat it. Mantras are not a magic cure. They shouldn't be used instead of prescribed medication from a medical practitioner. When it comes to our emotions, it is easier to explore alternative approaches because of the complexities of the mind. Mantras for physical healing are best used alongside medical recommendations.

Imagine you have a cold. The best thing is probably paracetamol, but you know that if you increase your vitamin C, you will help your body fight the symptoms. The mantras in this chapter are like an extra boost of vitamin C!

A QUICK REVIEW OF THE CHAKRAS

There are seven chakras in our body starting at the base of the spine with the last at the very top of our head. Each chakra is like a spinning wheel, energy enters one and then is driven up to the next, activating each one.

There are 7 bija sounds or seeds that with deep concentration and a focus on the sounds and vibrations that are created, can help to unblock the chakras and allow energy to flow throughout the body.

- Root Chakra – Lam
- Sacral Chakra – Vam
- Solar Plexus Chakra – Rum
- Heart Chakra – Yam
- Throat Chakra – Ham

- Third Eye Chakra – U
- Crown Chakra – Om

The root chakra is where our energy sits. The crown chakra is right at the top of our head, the closest point to a higher self and also the deities. It makes sense that the bija sound is Om.

Aside from these 7 principal sounds, there are also marmas, a sound that relates to various parts of the body, or marma. There are 50 in total, divided into the head, joints and limbs, abdominal area, and tissues and organs. The marmas are incredibly specific to regions of the body and one sound will alleviate symptoms in the left nostril while another will help free you from suffering in your right toes.

Mantras that activate the chakras and aim at healing certain parts of the body are only short sounds compared with some of the longer mantras we have now seen. Nevertheless, when you concentrate on the vibrations and direct those vibrations to the intended part of the body, there is great physical healing to be had.

A MANTRA TO PROTECT YOU FROM ALL DANGERS

Regardless of your culture and belief, most will agree that prevention is better than cure. For this, we turn to Lord Hanuman, who has many names, but you can see from his appearance why he is also called the monkey god. Despite his looks, there is nothing cheeky about him. He is considered by many as an incarnation of Lord Shiva and for this, is worshipped for numerous reasons.

One of the Hanuman mantras is intended for the protection against all dangers as well as provide you with additional strength, stamina, devotion, and wisdom. The Hanuman Gayatri mantra can also lead to more courage and help eliminate your doubts.

Om Anjaneyaya Vidmahe Vayuputraya Dhimahi
Tanno Hanumat Prachodayat

We pray to the son of Anjana and the son of the wind
go Vayu
May the Lord lead our intellect towards intelligence and
knowing

I wasn't the only one to appreciate the benefits. I used it from early September through to early January as I had always been prone to the winter bugs. Whether the group members were using it for just a few months or all year round, there were definitely fewer sniffles and coughs and the long dark days of winter were met with more strength and motivation.

A MANTRA FOR THE FATHER OF AYURVEDA MEDICINE

This is another excellent mantra that can be used to help get rid of various illnesses and suffering when used in the right way. Lord Dhanvantri is one of the manifestations of Lord Vishnu and is the ultimate healer. As well as alleviating the suffering from illnesses and diseases, he can help remove the fear we have of suffering and replace it with happiness.

The Lord Dhanvantri mantra is slightly different from the others we have seen because the success depends on a belief in the powers of this deity. Each time you chant it, a touch of his healing power reaches you. If a person doesn't believe in his ability to heal, they won't be blessed with his power. The more often you repeat this mantra, the more divine power will reach you.

It is also necessary for you to positively prepare your mind before chanting the Lord Dhanvantri mantra. I begin with a short English mantra to draw my focus and reinforce my determination to rid myself of the pain. You can choose your own words, just make sure they are in the present tense and they are positive. "I am getting better" when said with conviction, can enable this mantra to really ease any type of suffering.

Om Nano Bhagavate Vasudevaaya Dhanvantaraye Amrita-Kalasha Hastaaya Sarva-Amaya Vinashaaya Trailokya Naathaya Dhanvantri Maha-Vishnave Namha

I bow down to the Lord Dhanvantri, the Lord with four hands carrying a conch, discuss a leech and a pot of immortal nectar. In his heart shines a pleasing and brilliant blaze of light. The light is also seen shining around his head and beautiful lotus eyes. His divine play destroys all diseases like a blazing fire.

You would normally start with this mantra the full 108 times and then increase in multiples, so 216, 332, etc. It is also best to start before sunrise and continue as it rises. Many believe that with acts of kindness like donating to the poor, and using a crystal mala, you will see further benefits.

These benefits can include freedom from physical and emotional suffering, long-term illness, and even help others who are sick. Some have also noticed relief from symptoms when they have exhausted all medical options.

A TIBETAN MANTRA TO PURIFY THE BODY AND MIND

If you are looking for a shorter mantra that will help unblock physical and mental obstacles and clear away the parasitic thoughts and feelings we have, this mantra will allow you to rid yourself of negativity and improve your overall strength.

Om Ah Hum Soha

The sounds will help free ourselves from the guilt and shame of our negative actions (Om), from our negative words (Ah) and our negative thought (Hum), and Soha is Tibetan for "so be it".

When we chant this mantra, it is important to visualize specific colours in parts of your body. On the Om sound, imagine a bright white light in your brain. When you repeat Ah, see the colour red around your throat area. For the Hum, blue around your heart. The Soha isn't a colour word but it should help you to feel in the moment, letting things be as they are.

MY FORTUNATE MEETING WITH AN INCREDIBLE DOCTOR

As much as I wanted to visit patients in hospitals and introduce patients to healing mantras, I never felt that it was appropriate. It was like crossing a line that wasn't quite ready to be crossed. That is why I was ecstatic when a friend of a friend introduced me to a very open-minded doctor who was always looking for alternative ways to improve the quality of life of his patients. He was a strong believer that taking pets in to see patients helped with faster recovery and was keen to see if mantras could make a difference.

Together we looked at charts and discussed patients who were willing to try mantras alongside the treatment they were already receiving.

Incurable Diseases

When in Delhi, I met a pharmacist, so it was great to get an opinion from a medical believer. He introduced me to the Mhamirtunjya mantra of Lord Shiva and explained how it was one of the best mantras for those suffering from incurable diseases.

Om Haum Jum Sah- meaning Lord Shiva, give me life, fill me with life

Along with this mantra, you need a glass of water with two tulsi leaves, a drop of ganga water and a teaspoon of turmeric powder. When chanting, the water absorbs the vibrations of the sound and is then drunk.

We worked with various cancer patients, some were in the middle of chemotherapy, others had tried all that science could offer. The outcomes were inspiring. The patients suffered from less pain, they had an increased appetite and overall, regained a lot of their lost strength. Many of the patients who I still talk to have continued using the Mhamirtunjya mantra, years after our original meeting.

. . .

More assistance from Lord Hanuman

My doctor friend and I spent time in the clinic too, offering mantras for aches and pains, migraines, even pregnant women who wanted to improve their health and prepare for childbirth.

One case that caught my eye was a woman who had the flu literally every 6 to 8 weeks. She had changed her diet, increased her vitamins and tried to be more physically active when she could but nothing was making a difference. She was being tested for underlying medical conditions but at the same time, we worked together on a Hanuman mantra.

On Namo Bhagvate Aanjaneyaay Mahaabalayy Swaahaa

I bow down and surrender to Lord Hanuman, he who is the son of the powerful Anjana.

I actually encouraged many patients to use this mantra because it is good for not only infectious diseases but also diseases in general. Lord Hanuman helped restore Goddess Sita back to Sri Rama, so I felt this lady would gain form his restorative powers as well as his courage, which would help her continue with her healing. As a mantra that helps to remove disturbances we face in life, we also felt that it would help clear her mind in case this was impacting her immune system.

Two years later, after maintaining a healthy lifestyle and practising this mantra daily, she was free from her continuous bouts of the flu.

THE HEART MANTRA

Also known as the Great Heart of Wisdom Sutra, essentially, it refers to form as emptiness and is a key aspect of the four truths. There are various translations and can be used in different ways, but our intention was to help people alleviate the symptoms of heart disease.

Gate Gate Pāragate Pārasaṃgate Bodhi Svāhā

Gone, Gone, everyone gone to the other shore, awakening so be it

The mantra requires the visualization of the person moving to the shore but not actually leaving themselves. We worked together on images of the heart disease being taken to the shore and leaving behind what was essentially an empty heart, one not riddled with disease.

This mantra required great dedication and focus, so we also used an English mantra beforehand so that we could concentrate our heart and mind. We started with deep breathing exercises and repeated "My heart is pure".

Our group were not the only ones to experience significant improvements. Many studies have proven a link between anxiety and depression with chronic heart disease. One study included 41 people with acute coronary syndrome. Over 6 to 18 months, the impact of a 4-day spiritual retreat (which included meditation) was assessed with those who had various degrees of depression. Everyone was less depressed at the end of the study, but those who suffered from the highest levels of depression saw the greatest results.

When you feel like only a miracle will help

My stepfather was in the special forces, a lifetime ago as he would say but this gives you an idea of his physical strength. I always saw him as untouchable, nothing could stop him. Still, we started to notice him getting wobbly on his legs and shooting pains going down both sides. Doctors did all of the tests and discovered a pocket of fluid on his lower spine. He went ahead and had the surgery but unfortunately, after three months of physical therapy, there was no improvement.

He was not going to go in for chanting, but he agreed that if I really wanted to try, I could. I knew it would have to be a mantra that saw fast results if I was going to sway him.

Hang Hanumate Rudraatmakaay Hung Phatt

We bow to the highest principle, to Hanuman, the manifestation of the Reliever of suffering. Cut the ego! Purify! I am one with the god.

I was chuffed to bits when I got a phone call just a week later. His symptoms had almost disappeared. There was still the occasional jolt of pain, but he was back doing his DIY and even driving. I knew this mantra would provide him with the power he needed, and it was a relief to see this man so strong again.

A FINAL MANTRA FOR LONGEVITY

The Mahamrityunjaya mantra is one of the most powerful mantras to worship Lord Shiva. The vibrations can keep evil at bay and help restore well-being. It can help overcome negative emotions like jealousy and greed. If you chant it before going to sleep, it may even help prevent nightmares.

Most significantly, it can help rejuvenate your body and promote longevity, warding off death. With a profound belief in its powers and used in the right way, the Mahamrityunjaya mantra can bring your mind, body, and emotions into one.

You should chant this mantra with your palm completely covering a glass of water. The number 108 is essential, 1 representing self, 0 for nothing, and 8, the symbol of infinity. Once you have repeated it 108 times, you can drink the water or even use it as a spray for yourself or your home.

Aum Tryambakam Yajaamahe Sugandim Pushtivadhanam
Urvaarukamiva Bandhanaan-Mrityormuksheeya
Maamritaat

*We worship the three-eyed One, who is fragrant and who
nourishes all
Like the fruit falls off from the bondage of the stem, we will
be liberated from death and mortality*

While there is no possible way to prevent death, this mantra will help to prevent untimely death and the fear we have of dying.

It wasn't just the patients who benefited from the Mahamrityunjaya mantra, the families were also relieved of their suffering. It is extremely painful watching someone you love suffer, and this can often bring about an imbalance in emotions as well as physical problems. Most of the family members also felt rejuvenated, refreshed, and more positive after using this mantra.

Really, there are is an unlimited amount of power that can be unlocked when using mantras for physical healing. It is important that the user of each mantra is convinced that it is going to relieve them from suffering, whether that is for their own symptoms or somebody else's.

From skin disorders to broken bones, from cancer to heartburn, I have seen first-hand how mantras can help an array of people. It's not magic, but watching someone who had no hope of becoming stronger, to see them smile again and to start to enjoy life as they should, the only word to describe the feeling is magical!

CONCLUSION

We have reached the end of this particular journey together. Regardless of where you started, the challenges you faced, your beliefs, your age, or gender, you will now be able to take the knowledge from this book and begin to see the amazing benefits of healing mantras.

The importance of appreciating Hindu culture can't be stressed enough. It is such a pity that a culture and philosophy which has so much wisdom isn't more widely used or used in the wrong way. The language and traditions are so meaningful that with a true understanding of the power a single sound has, people are able to turn their lives around. Though English mantras can too have healing abilities, it's the sound and vibrations produced in Sanskrit that encourage the most healing and a higher connection to your inner self and the deities if you so choose.

One of the most significant things to bear in mind is that regardless of your situation, there will be a mantra, but before you randomly select one that you like the sound of or is a little bit easier to roll off the tongue, it is crucial that you strip back all of the layers of stress, pain, obstacles, and worries that you have in your life. You need to discover who you are in the present, not someone's mum or another one's assistant, just you.

From now on, there should be no more vague goals or desires. In order to choose the mantras that will lead to an improved life, you need to know exactly what your intentions are and where you want to go moving forward. Every person is an individual, so take the time to find out what makes you unique.

Remember the main goals of life according to Vedic thought; Dharna, Artha, Kama, and Moksha and how important that your goals are aligned with the gunas; Sattva, Tamas, and Rajas. When you know what you want to achieve based on your goals and intentions, you will be able to find the most relevant mantras for you.

The how, when, and where you practice your mantras will never be imposed on you, you can't make a mistake by sitting in the wrong position and enrage the gods or feed your negative karma. Most of the time, it is more important that you are comfortable so that you can concentrate. The Kundalini mantras require you to be sat up straight so that the energy at your spine can flow freely up to your mind. In an ideal world, you will be in a peaceful setting, but if that's not possible, as you continue to practise the mantras, your concentration will improve, and you will find it easier to block out the distractions of the world.

Most mantras are more effective when practised before sunrise, it's the perfect way to clear your mind, align your energies, and start the day with a positive outlook. If you aren't keen on rising as early as the sun, try to incorporate them into your morning routine before the stresses of the day begin. It is also recommended to repeat the mantras before going to bed to encourage a sound night's sleep.

Malas are a wonderful tool that can help you count the number of times you are repeating a mantra and this allows you to focus the mind on the sounds, vibrations, and in some cases, like the Shakti mantras, the area of the body that requires healing.

The glass of water is another amazing tool that will increase the power of the mantras. Don't forget that sound waves travel through water faster than air, so being in front of a glass of water or even covering one with your hand will transfer the sounds and vibrations to the water.

With regards to both emotional and physical healing, I do recommend using one or even a few of the mantras that prepare the body and mind. Diving straight into a mantra to heal a broken heart won't be as effective if you haven't prepared yourself to begin healing. Think of it as a warmup before going for a run.

I was so fortunate to watch people from my groups and patients in the hospital turn their lives around. The stories are based on real cases but naturally the names were changed. Though not religious, I can only say that sharing their experiences was a blessing and something I will always be grateful for. Following the journey of people like Shaun, Emma, and Sophie as they freed themselves from everything holding them back showed me that anyone who is willing can learn how to control their emotions, overcome anxiety and go after the things they want in life.

'Flu lady', my stepfather, and the hundreds of patients who were willing to try, despite previous bad experiences or being sceptical were able to get back on their feet. To go back to the life they thought they would never experience again, but this time, stronger and more determined.

You will notice that many mantras can be used for a variety of reasons and at first, you might struggle to see how the same set of words can achieve two completely different results. This again relates back to your intention of the mantra. Even after years of practice, make sure you are clear with your intentions and adjust your goals before finding a mantra so that the right powers and energies are produced.

You will also find that there may be different translations for the same mantra. Don't worry about this. Have you ever played the game 'whisper down the lane' where you whisper a word to a person, and they have to whisper it back until it reaches the last person? Look at mantras as a game of Whisper down the lane that has lasted for around 3000 years and you will see how the concept and meaning are there, but different teachers have translated it in different ways depending on their regional dialect.

Finally, it has been a great privilege sharing my learnings and experiences with you. So many years ago, I had no direction or motivation and I couldn't see my purpose in life. Without healing mantras, I could never have imagined finding the strength, confidence and passion to write a book like this. If you have enjoyed reading this, please leave a review on Amazon, if you purchased online, so that I can continue learning and for further insight you can read my other books on chakras and tarot cards. I truly hope that you to will be able to change your life for the better.

Thank you for reading my book. If you have enjoyed reading it perhaps you would like to leave a star rating and a review for me on Amazon? It really helps support writers like myself create more books. You can leave a review for me by scanning the QR code below:

Thank you so much. Verda Harper

REFERENCES

Dudeja, Jai. (2017). Scientific Analysis of Mantra-Based Meditation and its Beneficial Effects: An Overview. International Journal of Advanced Scientific Technologies in Engineering and Management Sciences. 3. 21. 10.22413/ijastems/2017/v3/i6/49101.

7 Simple Mantras for Healing and Transformation. (2019, October 2). Retrieved from https://chopra.com/articles/7-simple-mantras-for-healing-and-transformation

A. (n.d.). 18 Ways to Create Good Karma. Retrieved from https://chantamantra.com/index.php/articles/38-18-ways-to-create-good-karma

A. (2017, February 6). Practice the 12-Minute Yoga Meditation Exercise. Retrieved from https://alzheimersprevention.org/research/kirtan-kriya-yoga-exercise/

A. (2020a, April 24). 10 Powerful Mantras for Meditation - Dhyan Mantras. Retrieved from https://vedicfeed.com/ powerful-meditation-mantras/

A. (2020b, July 21). 15 Powerful Ganesh Mantras To Remove Obstacles & For Success. Retrieved from https://vedicfeed.com/ powerful-ganesh-mantras/

Alpert, Y. M. (2017, June 26). 13 Major Yoga Mantras to Memorize. Retrieved from https://www.yogajournal.com/ yoga-101/13-major-mantras-memorize#gid= ci020756a3b0142620&pid=majormantra9

Ashley-Farrand, T. (1999). Healing Mantras. Retrieved from https://books.google.es/books?id=zbKv3Jk-3YQC&pg= PA123&lpg=PA123&dq=how+long+does+it+take+for+ healing+mantras+to+work&source=bl&ots=GcKMeCxiDO& sig=ACfU3U2jCoNIy7VUb_0M1qtlsRyytOKfIQ&hl=en&sa= X&ved=2ahUKEwjEj- _Tu7bqAhXcA2MBHdqGBX0Q6AEwAHoECAkQAQ#v= onepage&q=how%20long%20does%20it%20take%20for% 20healing%20mantras%20to%20work&f=true

Astrology, T. (2019, August 5). Here's Why The Mahamrityun-jaya Mantra Is Chanted 108 Times For Lord Shiva. Retrieved from https://timesofindia.indiatimes.com/astrology/hindu-mythology/heres-why-the-mahamrityunjaya-mantra-is-chanted-108-times-for-lord-shiva/articleshow/70530345.cms

Ayurveda 101: The Three Doshas- Vata, Pitta, Kapha. (2014). Retrieved from http://www.eattasteheal.com/ ayurveda101/eth_bodytypes.htm

Ayurvedic Medicine and Therapies and Sunshine Coast. (n.d.). Retrieved from https://yuktibotanicals.vendecommerce.com/ pages/the-four-goals-of-life-according-to-ayurveda-purushartha

Castro, J. (2013, November 22). What Is Karma? Retrieved from https://www.livescience.com/41462-what-is-karma.html

Construction of the Vedas - VedicGranth.Org. (n.d.). Retrieved from https://sites.google.com/a/vedicgranth.org/www/ what_are_vedic_granth/the-four-veda/interpretation-and-more/construction-of-the-vedas?mobile=true-

Crowley, J. (2017, January 8). 3 Sanskrit Mantras to Boost Your Meditation Practice. Retrieved from https://www. yogiapproved.com/om/3-sanskrit-mantras-boost-meditation-practice/

Desk, F. W. (2019, August 18). Eka Vimshati Namavali of Ganpati: 21 names of Lord Ganesha with meaning and mantras. Retrieved from https://www.freepressjournal.in/webspecial/ eka-vimshati-namavali-of-ganpati-21-names-of-lord-ganesha-with-meaning-and-mantras

Digital, T. N. (2020, May 17). The Sun is an eternal source of energy; check out the benefits of chanting the Surya Mantras every morning. Retrieved from https://www.timesnownews. com/spiritual/religion/article/the-sun-is-an-eternal-source-of-energy-check-out-the-benefits-of-chanting-the-surya-mantras-every-morning/592967

Espada, J. (2020, March 24). Buddhist healing: strengthening health, helping others — downloadable text from Jason Espada: A Collection of Buddhist Methods for Healing. Retrieved from https://buddhaweekly.com/science-mantras-mantras-work-without-faith-research-supports-effectiveness-sanskrit-mantra-healing-even-environmental-transformation/

Frawley, D. (2010). Mantra Yoga and the Primal Sound. Retrieved   from   https://books.google.es/books?id= a1An08EBHCgC&pg=PA35&lpg=PA35&dq=how+can+ mantras+be+used+for+good+gunas&source=bl&ots= WYcl8cZnzG&sig= ACfU3U3ypcr_YV31mALnu3ifJmc9UchhgQ&hl=en&sa=X& ved= 2ahUKEwii5fukusXqAhULKBoKHVHKBjoQ6AEwCnoECAU QAQ#v=onepage&q=how%20can%20mantras%20be%20used% 20for%20good%20gunas&f=true

Guru Shakti. (2019, October 10). Retrieved from https://www. gurushakti.org.in/672/sadhna/success-in-life/brahma-mantra-

Hayter, S. W., & Jenny, H. (1977). Cymatics, Vol. II. Leonardo, 10(4), 334. Retrieved from https://monoskop. org/images/

7/78/Jenny_Hans_Cymatics_A_Study_of_Wave_Phenomena_a nd_Vibration.pdf

https://www.sivasakti.com/tantra/other-hindu-deities/shiva-the-god-of-destruction/. (n.d.). Retrieved from https://www.sivasakti.com/tantra/other-hindu-deities/shiva-the-god-of-destruction/

Luenendonk, M. (2019, September 25). These are the 10 Most Exciting Mantras for Meditation. Retrieved from https://www.cleverism.com/mantras-for-meditation/

Majumder, S. (2014, August 13). Why is Sanskrit so controversial? Retrieved from https://www.bbc.com/news/world-asia-28755509

mala beads. (2016, October 29). Retrieved from http://www.religionfacts.com/mala-beads

Mantra - New World Encyclopedia. (n.d.). Retrieved from https://www.newworldencyclopedia.org/entry/Mantra

Mark Gungor - The Nothing Box - Part 1. (2013, July 14). [Video file]. Retrieved from https://www.youtube.com/watch?v=SWiBRL-bxiA

Mark, J. J. (2020, July 22). The Vedas. Retrieved from https://www.ancient.eu/The_Vedas/

mindbodygreen. (2020a, January 30). The Transformative Powers of "Bija Mantra" Meditation. Retrieved from https://

www.mindbodygreen.com/0-5930/The-Transformative-Powers-of-Bija-Mantra-Meditation.html

mindbodygreen. (2020b, April 23). ROYGBIV: Your Guide To The 7 Chakra Colors & How To Use Them. Retrieved from https://www.mindbodygreen.com/articles/7-chakra-colors-what-they-mean-and-why-they-matter

N. (2020c, July 1). 10 Powerful Vishnu Mantras You Should Chant. Retrieved from https://vedicfeed.com/powerful-vishnu-mantra-to-chant/

NursingAnswers.net. (2020, February 11). Mantra, Music and Reaction Times: Its Applied Aspects. Retrieved from https://nursinganswers.net/essays/mantra-music-reaction-times-study-applied-9478.php

Ochsner, J. (2014). Meditation and Coronary Heart Disease: A Review of the Current Clinical Evidence. Retrieved from https://www.ncbi.nlm.nih.gov/pmc/articles/PMC4295748/

OM AH HUM Meditation. (2018, June 29). Retrieved from https://www.lamayeshe.com/article/om-ah-hum-meditation

Om Apavitrah Pavitro Va - In sanskrit with meaning. (n.d.). Retrieved from https://greenmesg.org/stotras/vishnu/om_apavitrah_pavitro_va.php

Prabhu, M. U. (2018, August 10). Mantra Yoga & Shakti Mantras. Retrieved from https://www.vedanet.com/mantra-yoga-primal-sound/

Pradīpaka, G. (n.d.). Learning Sanskrit - Sacred Mantra-s - Hrim - Sanskrit & Trika Shaivism. Retrieved from https://www.sanskrit-trikashaivism.com/en/learning-sanskrit-sacred-mantra-s-hrim/476-

Purushartha: The 4 Aims of Human Life. (2019, December 10). Retrieved from https://chopra.com/articles/purushartha-the-4-aims-of-human-life

ReShel, A. (2018, June 12). The Power of Nāda Yoga. Retrieved from https://upliftconnect.com/the-power-of-nada-yoga/

Sakhare, P. (2020, April 14). Green Tara Mantra: Om Tare Tuttare Ture Soha - Learn How to Say It. Retrieved from https://www.yowangdu.com/tibetan-buddhism/green-tara-mantra.html

Sankar, G. (2015, November 25). Spirituality: Chant Dhanvantri Mantra for healing, good health. Retrieved from https://zeenews.india.com/entertainment/and-more/spirituality-chant-dhanvantri-mantra-for-healing-good-health_1826074.html

Search Results for "Gayatri pronunciation" –. (n.d.). Retrieved from https://neensnotes.com/?s=Gayatri+pronunciation&submit=Search

User, S. (n.d.). Daily Vedic Family Prayer. Retrieved from https://aryasamajhouston.org/resources/articals/daily-vedic-family-prayer

Vilhauer, J. (2019, June 29). Mantra: A Powerful Way to Improve Well Being. Retrieved from https://www.psychologytoday.com/us/blog/living-forward/201906/mantra-powerful-way-improve-your-well-being

What are Affirmations? (n.d.). Retrieved from http://powerthoughtsmeditationclub.com/what-are-affirmations/

What is the meaning of the mantra Om haum joom sah? How does it work? - Quora. (n.d.). Retrieved from https://www.quora.com/What-is-the-meaning-of-the-mantra-Om-haum-joom-sah-How-does-it-work%20/

Wikipedia contributors. (2020, June 25). Karma in Hinduism. Retrieved from https://en.wikipedia.org/wiki/Karma_in_Hinduism

Wray, A. (2014, November 20). Mantra 101 – How To Choose a Mantra. Retrieved from https://www.malacollective.com/blogs/mala-collective/15766480-mantra-101-how-to-choose-a-mantra

Made in the USA
Monee, IL
04 February 2021